making rag rugs

making rag rugs

15 step-by-step projects

General Editor: Clare Hubbard
Introduction by Juju Vail

Storey Publishing

The mission of Storey Publishing is to serve our customers by publishing practical information that encourages independence in harmony with the environment.

North American edition published in 2002 by Storey Publishing, 210 MASS MoCA Way, North Adams, Massachusetts 01247

United Kingdom edition published in 2002 by
New Holland Publishers (UK) Ltd,
Garfield House, 86–88 Edgware Road,
London W2 2EA

10 9 8 7 6 5 4 3

Library of Congress Cataloging-in-Publication Data

Making rag rugs : 15 step-by-step projects / general editor, Clare Hubbard ; introduction by Juju Vail.
                    p. cm.
ISBN 978-1-58017-455-8 (alk. paper)
1. Rag rugs. 2. Hand weaving — Patterns. I. Hubbard, Clare.
TT850 M314 2002
746.7—dc21

Senior Editor: Clare Hubbard
Editor: Krystyna Mayer
Design: Fiona Roberts at Design Revolution Ltd
Photographer: Shona Wood
Production: Hazel Kirkman
Editorial Direction: Rosemary Wilkinson

Reproduction by Modern Age Repro House Ltd, Hong Kong
Printed and bound in Malaysia by Times Offset (M) Sdn. Bhd.

DISCLAIMER
The information in this book has been carefully researched and all efforts have been made to ensure accuracy. The author and publishers assume no responsibility for any injuries, damage, or losses incurred in connection with the use of information in this book.

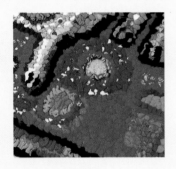

Contents

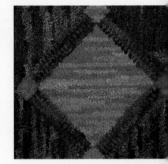

Projects

INTRODUCTION

The rug is one of the first things we look at when we come into a room. It plays a pivotal role in any decoration scheme and its color, pattern, and texture can be used to set design themes. Its shape can also influence the way you use a room, designating different areas and directing the flow of traffic. Yet it is difficult to find exactly the shape, color, size, and pattern that will provide the kind of impact that you desire without having a rug custom made at an exorbitant price. By making a rug yourself, you can have control over all the design elements. Moreover, if you make a rug out of rags, it will cost you hardly anything at all.

Rag-rug making is a traditional craft. In Britain and North America the techniques that were most commonly used were hooking, prodding, braiding, and weaving. The most common rag rug is a hooked rug, which has small loops of rag that have been drawn up through a burlap background. The pile is usually short and the design is clear to see. A prodded or clipped rug (they look the same, but employ a slightly different technique) has a shaggy pile. A braided rug is made of braids of fabric that have been joined together. These methods are now enjoying a revival, inspired partly by the desire to transform recycled materials into unique, handcrafted pieces for the home.

There is much speculation about whether the technique of hooking and prodding rags through burlap began in Britain and was brought to North America by settlers, or whether it originated in North America. Burlap was first imported to Britain and North America around 1850, and the oldest surviving examples of hooked rag rugs, dating from about that time, come from the eastern United States and from Quebec and the Maritime Provinces of Canada. Earlier examples, however, have been found in North America, where linen with some of its warp and weft threads removed was used in place of burlap.

Many wonderful examples of old rag rugs have survived, particularly in North America, where the craft was very popular. Made from old feed sacks, they usually measured about 32 x 44 in. (80 x 110 cm). A house typically had some rugs with utilitarian designs that were used every day and some that were reserved for the parlor or for special guests. For everyday use, designs of swirling lines made up of odd ends of rags were very common in what were called mishmash rugs. Checks and other geometric designs were also popular because they could be drawn on to the burlap without making special templates. These styles often seem most compatible with modern interiors.

Many of the treasured rugs that were reserved for special occasions have survived because they were kept away from household traffic. There is a great deal of variation in their designs. Printed designs of flowers, animals, and boats were often employed; no two of these designs looked exactly the same because the rags that were used always varied. Other designs were inspired by the imagination of their makers and included combinations of geometric shapes, animals, slogans, people, houses, and many other scenes.

Rag rugs have an enduring appeal. The techniques for making them are easily mastered and the abundance of materials that can be used is readily available and inexpensive. The techniques used in this book include hooking, prodding, clipping, and braiding. They require very little equipment and in no more than a couple of hours you will be working at a regular speed.

The opening chapter explains the general techniques. You can use these to design and make your own rug to fit your particular setting, or you can follow one of the project patterns designed for contemporary interiors. Of course, the rags that you find will inspire your own personal variations, ensuring that your rug is unique.

MATERIALS

Much of the pleasure of making rag rugs comes from finding the materials. Fabrics that look unattractive in an old item of clothing are transformed when included in a rag rug. Rag materials are widely available and inexpensive, but it is impossible to predict what you will find; this is what makes each rug unique. Old clothes, household textiles, and wrappings are all good sources. Fabrics that you can use include sweaters (particularly old shrunken ones in which the wool has felted), blankets, curtains, towels, nets, yarns, twisted newspaper, plastic bags, fur, feathers, candy wrappers, dresses, jackets, coats, t-shirts, and socks.

While any material can be used in a rag rug, certain fabrics make it easier to carry out the techniques. Hooked rugs are easiest to make if the rag material has a lot of give and some loft; thus knitted fabrics are much easier to work with than stiff, heavy ones. The best materials include t-shirts, wool sweaters, synthetic knits, lightweight cottons, nets, and plastic bags. Heavy woven wools may also be suitable, but the rag strips need to be thinner. Very heavy, stiff fabrics, such as new denim, are difficult to hook and are more suitable for prodded rugs, where a firm fabric is preferable. When making a braided rug, avoid fabrics that fray easily and, when selecting materials, bear in mind that the pattern on a fabric will be visible.

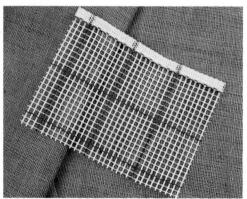

Top: balls of rags; *above:* rug canvas and burlap.

QUANTITY OF RAG FABRIC

The amount of fabric needed to make a rug depends on the technique to be used, the thickness of the fabric, and the length and density of the pile (if there is one). It is best to collect a wide variety of fabrics in your chosen colors, say a large bag full, and to add more fabric if you need it as you work. If you are hooking or prodding a rug, you can work out a rough estimate of how much fabric you will need by cutting a 20 x 20 in. (50 x 50 cm) piece of material that is typical of the type of fabric that you intend to use. Work the fabric square, then measure the worked patch and divide the size of the finished rug by the size of the patch. Multiply that number by 40 to arrive at the number of square inches of fabric you will need.

If you are using one particular fabric in a large area, you may find it difficult to obtain enough fabric from a single second-hand garment. You could buy either new material or several fabrics or pieces of clothing of a similar color and blend them together. You could also dye new or old fabric with a commercial dye.

BASE FABRIC

Hooked and prodded rugs require a base fabric to hold the rug pile. Traditionally the base fabric has been burlap, which comes in different weights (or thread counts) and different colors. The most common weights are 8, 10, and 12 ounces. The weight corresponds to the thread count (sometimes called the epi) which is the number of warp threads per inch. The higher the thread count (usually the lighter the weight) the denser the fabric will be. An 8-ounce burlap may have 10 warp threads per inch and is most suitable for a finely hooked rug, while a 12-ounce burlap has a loose weave and will be the easiest to use with a spring clip tool, as you need some room to maneuver the tool. A 10-ounce burlap is the most versatile and commonly used weight for the base fabric. Burlap is available in either a natural beige color or it is dyed in a variety of colors. In most cases, you will not see the base so the color is unimportant.

Although all the hooked, prodded, and clipped rugs in this book could be made using burlap as a base fabric, some crafters have used rug canvas, particularly for the prodded and clipped rugs. Rug canvas is not the same as painting or sailing canvas. It is a stiff fabric with enlarged holes between the warp and the weft threads. You do not need to use a frame to make a rug with rug canvas, but the rug will need a coating of adhesive on the back to hold the rag strips in place.

BACKING FABRIC

When completed, rugs may be backed either with burlap or with printed, dyed, or plain cotton fabrics. You can also use twill tape in a suitable color to edge the circumference of the backing.

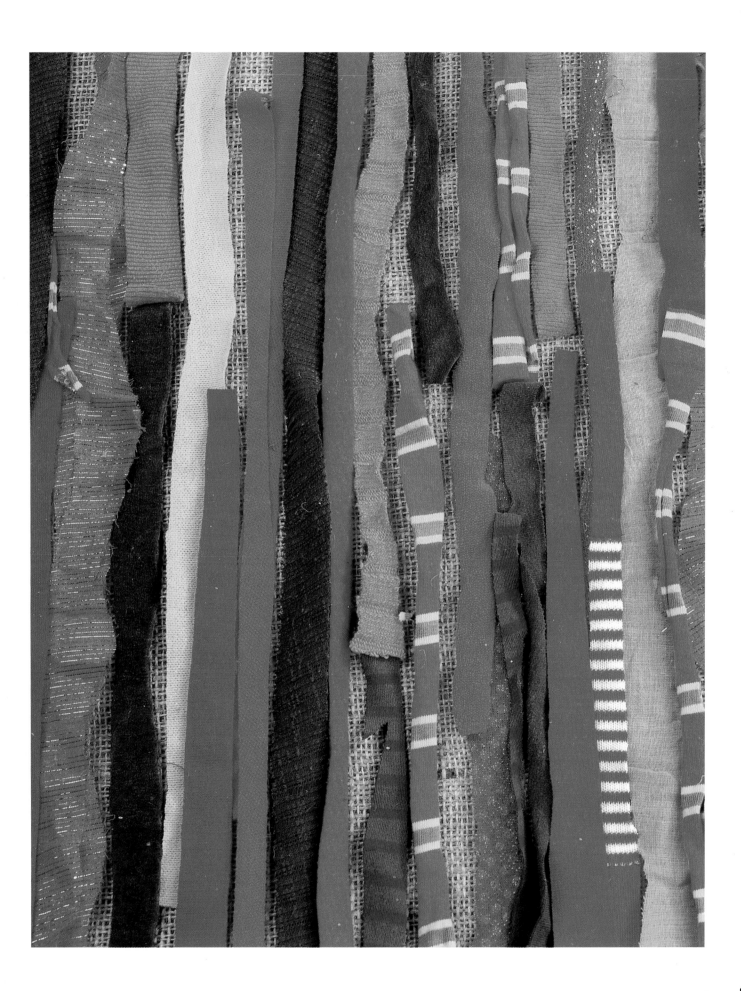

TOOLS & EQUIPMENT

Rag-rug making requires very little equipment and none that is expensive. Some tools, however, may not be readily available; rag-rug hooks and prodding tools are not usually sold in craft stores and may need to be ordered from a specialty supplier (see pages 78–79).

The tools and equipment needed depend on which rag-rug technique you are using – a braided rug requires little more than a needle, while a hooked rug requires a hook, frame, and scissors. In this book, the specific equipment needed is listed with each project. The various tools that can be used for each technique are described below, as is the equipment that is common to all of the techniques.

The one item that is essential to all techniques is a good pair of *heavy scissors*. You may also want to use a *cutting mat* and a *rotary cutter* for cutting the rag strips. This makes the job of cutting many strips of fabric much faster and easier on the hands than if you were using scissors. A *tape measure* is useful, as is a *yardstick*, for drawing the rug dimensions and pattern grids onto the burlap. *Pins*, *safety pins*, *needles*, and *thread* are useful for stitching linings to rugs.

HOOKED & PRODDED RUGS

To start with, you will need a thick *permanent marker* for drawing the rug design onto the burlap. If you do a lot of rug making and like to make detailed designs, you may want to invest in a *projector*, which can be used to enlarge the paper design to the size of the rug.

Traditionally, hooked and prodded rugs are made with burlap on a *frame*. A 20 x 20 in. (50 x 50 cm) canvas stretcher frame, available from art supply stores, is a good frame to start with because it makes a rug portable and easy to remount as the burlap slackens. You will need a *staple gun* suitable for wood to mount the burlap onto the canvas stretcher frame and a *staple remover*.

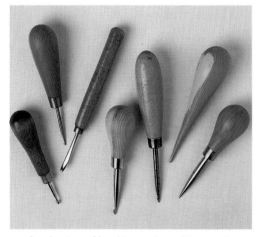

A selection of hooking and prodding tools.

If you want to work on a number of projects at once, you may find it worthwhile to invest in a purpose-built rug frame. This is available from mail-order suppliers (see pages 78–79).

A canvas stretcher can be used as a frame for hooking by resting most of the frame on a table, but for larger frames and prodded rugs you will need to support the frame on a pair of waist-high *trestles*. These need to be secured with *G-clamps*.

To make a hooked rug you need a *hook*. A rag-rug hook has a short, rounded handle with a crochet-type hook on the end. The handle fits into the palm of your hand. (If you were to use a crochet hook, the end would jab your palm uncomfortably.) A hook with a latch is also unsuitable. Rug hooks generally come in two sizes: primitive and extra-fine. Primitive hooks are commonly used for hooking rags. A fine hook is more suitable for wool yarns and very finely cut wool flannel. These hooks can be purchased through mail-order suppliers (see pages 78-79).

Prodding tools are used for making prodded rugs. Anything that can poke rag strips through the burlap can be used. A knitting needle or a bradawl are adequate, but purpose-made wooden and steel prodding tools are easier to use and can be bought through mail-order suppliers. You can also use a *spring clip tool* to achieve the same look with a slightly different technique. Unlike prodded rugs, clippers are worked with the right side of the rug facing you.

You may want to coat the back of a prodded or hooked rug with a *latex adhesive* to improve its durability and make it less slippery. Latex adhesives are sold in hardware stores for gluing carpet tiles to the floor. An old credit card or piece of heavy cardboard is perfect for spreading the latex over the backing.

1 – yardstick	5 – tape measure	9 – staple remover	13 – permanent markers
2 – pins	6 – cutting mat	10 – spring clip tool	14 – rotary cutter
3 – frame	7 – heavy scissors	11 – prodding tool	15 – staple gun
4 – latex adhesive	8 – needles and thread	12 – hook	

TRANSFERRING THE RUG DESIGN

To make the hooked, prodded, and clipped rugs in this book you will need to transfer the designs on to burlap or rug canvas. You may want to draw them freehand, which will be the easiest method for the simple geometric designs. Use two different colored markers so that you can make corrections. Start by drawing the design with a jumbo red marker, then stand back and look at the pattern. Make corrections with a bold black marker, then trace over the entire design with the black marker.

Often the easiest way to transfer a design is to make templates of the main motifs. Motifs can be enlarged on a photocopier, then cut out and reassembled (if they are larger than the paper) and pinned to the burlap. Stand back and look at the design. When you are happy with the placement, trace around the motifs with a marker pen, using a different color marker for any corrections (1).

If the rug design is more complicated or, as a beginner, you are slightly hesitant, you will need to enlarge the design on a grid (or with a projector). To enlarge a design using a grid, place a grid drawn on acetate on top of the design (2). With a marker, draw a grid onto the burlap that bears the same ratio to the acetate grid as the finished rug does to the design (3). Following the grid, copy the design onto the burlap with a marker pen, using a different color marker to correct any mistakes (4).

When positioning the design onto the burlap or canvas, leave a margin of 6 in. (15 cm) around the outside of the rug to allow for a hem and for stapling to the stretcher frame.

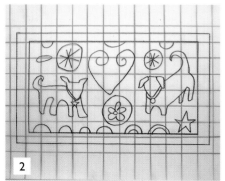

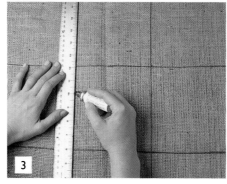

PREPARING THE RAGS

If you are using old clothes and materials for rug making, it is a good idea to machine-wash them on a hot cycle, then tumble dry. (Wool items may felt during this process, which will actually make them even better to work with.) Fabric softener will help make the rags more workable. New materials should also be cleaned to remove finishes.

To prepare the rag strips for hooking and prodding, remove any seams, buttons, zippers, and other notions from the garments (1, 2, and 3). If you have a rotary cutter, it is very easy to cut the material into strips of roughly equal width (4). If you are using scissors, you may want to fold the garment pieces so that you can cut through more than one layer at a time (5). The width of the strips will depend on which technique you choose, the material, and your personal preference. As a rough guide, try using strips about 1 in. (2 cm) wide for a medium-weight t-shirt material, or ½ in. (1 cm) wide for a lightweight wool sweater. Experiment to find your own preferences. Sort the rags into different color groups and store them in clear plastic bags, so that you can find the appropriate fabrics easily.

If you like the look of aged rugs, you may want to immerse the rag fabrics in a tea, coffee, or onion bath to mellow their colors.

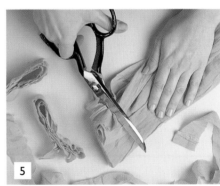

USING A STRETCHER FRAME

Most hooked and prodded rugs are made on a frame to keep the burlap taut. However, rugs worked on rug canvas do not need to be mounted on a frame to keep the base fabric taut, as it is already very stiff. Some people hook burlap-backed rugs without a frame since this makes their work more portable; but this can make the hooking slower and cause discomfort in the back and shoulders. If you use a small canvas stretcher frame, the rug will be easy enough to move around. An embroidery hoop is not suitable because it is not strong enough.

The rug frame will probably be much smaller than the size of the rug. It is usually best to start hooking or prodding in the middle and move the frame around as you need to; the burlap will become increasingly less taut as you work and will need restretching anyway.

If you buy a frame specially designed for rug making, the manufacturer's instructions will best describe how to attach the burlap, but if you want to make your own frame, buy a set of canvas stretchers and make a frame of about 20 x 20 in. (50 x 50 cm) (1). Begin by laying the burlap flat on the floor and positioning the frame on top. Fold the burlap over the frame along one side and staple it at one corner, then staple the fabric at the center and at the second corner of the frame. Add more staples at 1-in. (2 cm) intervals between the three staples. Pulling the fabric as taut as possible, stretch the burlap over the opposite edge of the frame. Fold it back over the edge and staple it at the center of that side (2). Then moving 1 in. (2 cm) to the right of the center staple, again pull the fabric as taut as possible and staple it. Move to the left of the center staple and repeat this process, stapling at 1-in. (2 cm) intervals and finishing with a staple in each corner. Continue in the same manner along the other sides of the frame, pulling the fabric taut as you work.

Once you have completed a section of the rug, you will need to pull out the staples with the staple remover and repeat this process. You may have to staple the rug through the pile. Pull the pile aside so that you staple only the burlap to the frame.

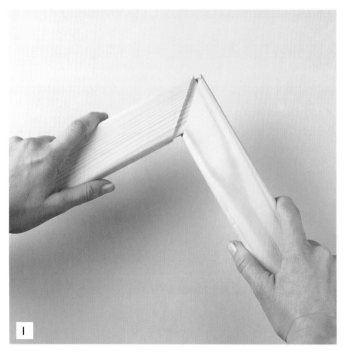

HOOKING

The rag strips in a hooked rug are not held in place by any kind of knot. They stay securely in the rug because the warp and weft threads of the burlap become displaced by the rag thickness and squeeze the pile in place.

Once you have stretched the burlap onto the frame and prepared some rag materials, sit comfortably at a table with the main part of the frame balancing on the table and part of it extending off the table, so that you can position one hand under the frame. Alternatively, support all four corners of the frame on trestles, using G-clamps. The rug should be about halfway between your waist and chest when you are seated.

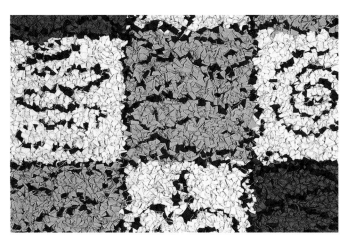

The Sardines rug (see pages 45–47) is made using the hooking technique.

2 Poke the hook through the weave of the burlap and grab the strip with the hook. This photograph shows what is happening on the underside of the rug.

1 Hooked rugs are made with the right side facing you. Use your writing hand to hold the hook above the burlap. Beneath the burlap, use the thumb and forefinger of your other hand to hold the cut strip ready to guide into the hook. The arm under the burlap should be bent at the elbow. If you are stretching into the middle of the frame, you may get a backache, so try to maintain good posture as you work. Move the burlap to a different position on the frame to avoid reaching too far.

3 Pull the end of the strip up through the weave to the top of the rug, being careful not to grab any of the burlap in the hook, so that you have a tail of at least ½ in. (1 cm).

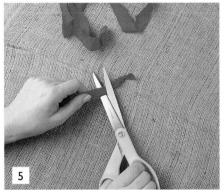

4 Poke the hook back down into a different gap in the warp and weft that is next to (or near) the rag end and pull a loop to the top of the burlap. A loop of between ¼ in. (0.5 cm) and ½ in. (1 cm) is standard for most 'primitive-style' hooking, but you can experiment with this to achieve a look you like. Repeat the process by poking the hook near the last loop and drawing up another loop.

5 When ending a row of hooking, pull the remainder of the strip through to the right side. Trim the ends of the strip to match the rest of the pile height. You may need to practice for 30 minutes or so before you can avoid pulling the burlap threads along with the strip, but you should be able to work quite quickly once you have mastered this step.

6 Make sure that you hook a pile dense enough to displace the threads in the weave of the burlap, otherwise the rag strips will pull out easily. However, the pile may be too densely hooked if it becomes hard to pull the rag loops up. Continue hooking until the burlap surface is covered. You can hook in parallel lines or concentric circles or outline your motifs.

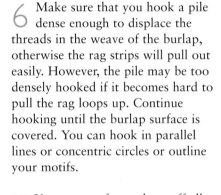

7 You may prefer to shear off all the loops. This will give you a smoother, denser-looking pile. To do this, wait until you have completed a couple of inches, then press the pile upwards with your hand below the burlap and clip the pile with a strong pair of scissors.

PRODDING

Prodded rugs have a long, shaggy pile, which is achieved by poking rag strips down through the burlap. For this reason, they are worked with the underside of the rug facing you. If you are using burlap, it must be stretched taut on a frame as explained on page 14. Prodded rugs are easiest to work if the frame is clamped to trestles, but they may also be worked with most of the frame resting on a table. To prepare the rags for prodding, cut a number of fabric strips measuring about 1 x 3½ in. (2 x 9 cm).

Perfect your prodding technique by making the Lavender Field rug (see pages 27–29).

1 Working with the underside of the rug facing you, use the prodding tool to force a small hole in between the weave of the burlap.

2 Push through one end of the strip of rag fabric.

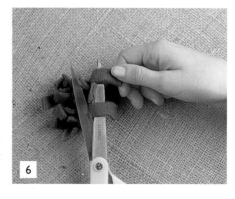

3 Move along about ¼ in. (0.5 cm) and make another opening in the weave of the burlap. Push through the other end of the rag strip.

4 With the hand that is not holding the prodding tool, guide the rag strip through the underside of the burlap, pulling the ends of the strip until they are even in length. This photograph shows the right side of the rug at this stage.

5 Prod a second strip of fabric through the rug in the same way, about ¼ in. (0.5 cm) from the last one. Continue prodding until the surface of the rug is covered and no burlap can be seen on the right side of the rug.

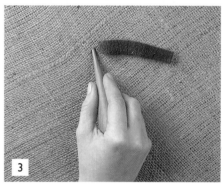

6 When the prodding is complete, check that the pile is even and trim any long ends, if necessary.

CLIPPING

A clipped rug looks the same as a prodded rug but is made using a different tool. Stretch the burlap on a frame and prepare the rags in the same way as for prodded rugs. Work the rug with the right side facing you and both hands above the surface.

The colorful Shag Rug, shown on pages 48–50, is made using the clipping technique.

1 With the clip closed, push the tool down through the weave of the burlap and then up about ¼ in. (0.5 cm) away.

2 Open the clip and grab one end of the rag strip.

3 Hold the other end of the rag in your free hand, then pull the clip back through the burlap. Adjust the ends of the rag so that they are equal.

4 Continue in this manner until the surface of the rug is covered and no burlap can be seen on the right side of the rug.

5 Trim any pile that is uneven.

BRAIDING

Sewing braided rags together is a traditional way of creating a rag rug. This can be done in many different ways. The most common design is a coiled braid that forms a circular or an oval shape. Other shapes can be made by creating clusters of small, coiled braids, which are then edged with a larger braid. Shorter pieces can be placed next to each other to make rectangular rugs.

The width of braiding strips can vary depending on the type of fabric you use and how chunky you want the rug to be. It is best to choose fabrics that are of a similar weight, keeping fabrics of light weights for one rug and woolens for another. If the weight does vary slightly, compensate for this by cutting wider strips of the finer fabric.

Begin by making a small sample with your chosen materials to see if you like the thickness. To prepare braids for a coiled rug, cut rag strips about 2 in. (5 cm) wide and as

Use the braiding technique to create the Braided Wool rug on pages 42–44.

long as possible. If the pieces are too short (under a yard) you will have to do a lot of stitching to join them together. Fasten the ends of three strips of fabric together with a safety pin and hook the pin over a cup hook screwed into something secure just above eye level. As you braid, fold in the raw edges of the rags so that they are concealed within the folded strips. Start braiding near the pin by bringing the right-hand strip over the middle strip, then the left-hand strip over the new middle strip. Continue braiding, turning the raw edges inside (1). When you are about to run out of rag, sew on a new strip and trim the seam to ¼ in. (0.5 cm). Make sure you stagger these seams to avoid lumps in the braids. When you are done, secure the loose ends with a pin.

To make a coiled rug, use a carpet needle and heavy linen thread to sew first through the loop of one braid, then through the loop lying beside it. Work backward and forward between the braids, coiling as you go and taking care that the braids remain flat and that the stitching is firm but not too tight (2). Continue until the rug is the desired size.

To achieve a smooth finish on the edge of the rug, taper the last 10 in. (25 cm) of each strip to about half the normal width. Finish the braiding and slip the tapered ends into the loop lying beside them. Secure the ends in place, hiding the raw edges.

DESIGNING YOUR OWN RUG

Once you have practiced these techniques and gained some confidence, the next step is to design your own rug. You may get ideas from textile collections in museums, paintings, drawings, or books that feature textiles and other decorative patterns. You may want to design a rug for a specific room and take your inspiration from its decor. Hooked, prodded, and clipped rugs can be made in any shape; you could, for instance, design a rug to hug a piece of furniture, such as a chair, or to direct the flow of traffic around a room. Think about the existing colors and patterns in the room. You may want to use a motif from another fabric in the room, changing its scale to make a different impact.

Draw your idea on a piece of paper the size of the rug you want to make and stand above it. Remember that the design will be viewed from different directions, so check it from all angles. Does the scale of the motif seem overpowering or too small? Is the rug the right size or does it seem to be lost among the furniture? You may want to trace the outlines of all the dominant shapes of the design onto a second piece of paper, then use them as templates to cut out shapes in the colors you are considering. Place these on top of the original drawing to get an idea of how the color scheme and value balance looks within the room. Play around until you achieve a design that pleases you.

FINISHING & CLEANING

Coating the back of a rug with a latex adhesive will prevent it from unraveling and make it firmer and less slippery. This can be done to rugs made with any technique, but it is best for hooked, prodded, and clipped rugs. Braided rugs benefit from being reversible and a latex backing prevents that.

Latex adhesive can be bought in hardware stores as a carpet-tile adhesive. Squeeze some onto the back of the rug and spread it around with an old credit card or a heavy piece of cardboard, pushing it into the gaps as you work. When you have finished coating the back of the entire rug with latex adhesive (it will appear white before drying to a clear finish), fold down the hem of the rug and press it into the

latex. Leave it to dry for 24 hours in a well-ventilated room. Cut the backing fabric to the same size as the finished rug plus 2 in. (5 cm) on all sides to allow for a hem. Press the hem under with a hot iron, then pin the backing over the reverse of the rug. Whipstitch the backing into place. Pin the twill tape over the hem seam and stitch it into place. You may wish to apply another coat of latex adhesive to the back to prevent the rug from slipping on a wooden floor. See the individual projects for other ways to back rugs.

Clean a finished rag rug by vacuuming it with a low suction. If the rug becomes soiled, the best way to clean it is by dabbing the stain with a clean, damp cloth until the stain is gone. Never submerge the rug in water.

HOW TO USE THIS BOOK

The projects in this book have been chosen to both instruct the beginner and to inspire the established rag-rug enthusiast. All of the projects are distinct and focus on a different area of rug making, such as using color, combining techniques, adding appliquéd elements, and transferring a pictorial pattern onto burlap. Although the projects have not been formulated as a course to be strictly followed, they have been ordered from simple to more complex. If you are a beginner, it is advisable that you complete some of the earlier projects before attempting the more ambitious designs.

You should also read through the introductory pages thoroughly, as detailed descriptions of the basic techniques are not repeated in the projects. If you begin to work on a project and find there's something that you've forgotten or you need more information, refer back to those pages and you will find the answer.

Every project is clearly described and provides all of the information that you need. A detailed 'you will need' list, step-by-step instructions with accompanying color illustrations, and full-color photographs of the finished rug with close-up details bring the projects to life and make them easy to do.

An at-a-glance 'specifications' box gives you the size of the rug and the technique(s) used, so you will automatically know whether the rug is the right size and has the right look for your decor. Examples of these elements are shown below and at right.

Each project comes with a helpful diagram and templates, if appropriate. Because most of the rugs are simple or geometric in design, it shouldn't be necessary for you to enlarge the diagrams. They are there for you as a guide and are not shown at a specific scale. Many have a grid already placed on them, or you can draw a grid and place it over the diagram if that helps you. Instructions for how to enlarge templates are described on page 12.

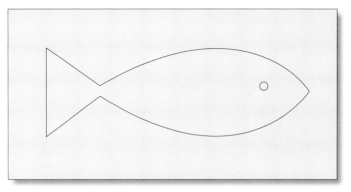

Template

Diagram

> **SPECIFICATIONS**
>
> *Rug size:* 60 x 36 in.
> (150 x 90 cm)
> *Technique:* Clipping (see page 18)

Specification box

The satisfaction of making a rag rug is that there aren't any strict rules that need to be followed, you only need to know the basic techniques. Enjoy the creative freedom that this craft provides.

Step-by-step
illustration

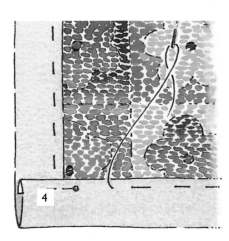

4

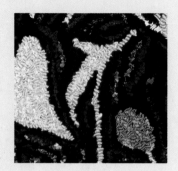

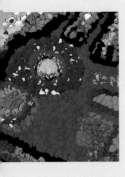

Projects

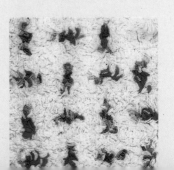

Retro Flowers
Sara Worley

This very simple and cheerful hooked rug was inspired by the classic flower shape used in designs by Andy Warhol and Mary Quant in the 1960s. Four main colors of fabric were used, plus a touch of a dark color for the center of the flowers.

1 Enlarge the flower template by 190% and trace it onto tracing paper. Transfer the design onto cardboard, then place the cardboard on a cutting mat and cut it out with a craft knife.

2 Referring to the diagram on page 26, measure and draw the grid onto the burlap with a marker pen (each square is 8 in./20 cm). Center the flower template in each square and draw around it using the marker pen.

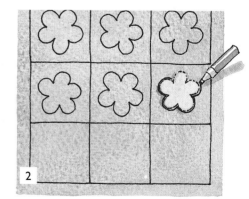

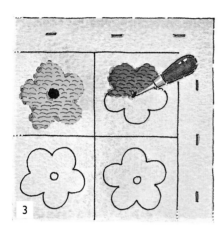

3 Mark a dot in the middle of each flower. Attach the burlap to the frame, making sure that it is taut. Hook in the strips of fabric – you can either follow the design shown or devise your own color scheme. First fill in the flowers and then the backgrounds of the squares until the rug is complete.

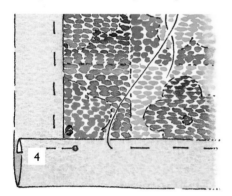

4 Remove the rug from the frame and place it face down on the floor. Turn in a double hem of about 2 in. (5 cm) to the wrong side of the rug and pin it all the way around. Fold and pin the corners neatly. Sew the hem to the back of the rug with the wool thread.

> **KEY**
> A = 24 in. (60 cm)
> B = 48 in. (120 cm)
> C = 8 in. (20 cm)

> **MAKER'S TIP**
> *I prefer not to back my rugs because dirt can become trapped between the layers and I do not like using latex adhesives because they can sometimes discolor with age.*

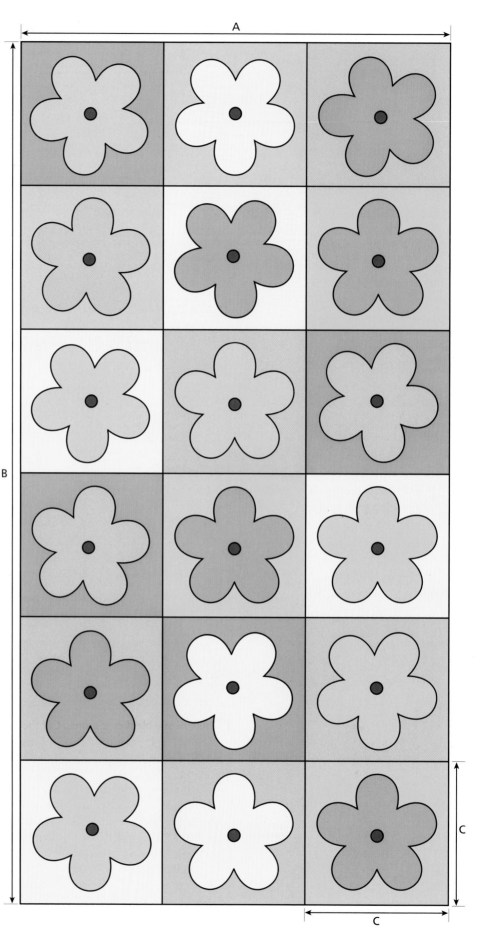

Lavender Field
Maureen Green

The inspiration for this rug came from a visit to the lavender fields in Norfolk, England. I used soft wool blankets dyed in shades of green and mauve to represent the lavender flowers, foliage, and surrounding fields. Dried lavender flower heads were sewn into the lining to provide a scented natural alternative to room fresheners.

You will need

- Scissors
- 3 pale-colored wool blankets, single size
- Large pan or dye bath
- Commercial dyes in mauve, dark green, and pale green
- Sewing machine and thread
- 2 pieces 10-oz. burlap, each 52 x 36 in. (130 x 90 cm)
- Marker pen
- Tape measure
- Graph paper
- Frame
- Rotary cutter (optional)
- Cutting mat (optional)
- Prodding tool
- 2 pieces iron-on interfacing or bonding (optional), each 46 x 30 in. (115 x 75 cm)
- Dried lavender flower heads (optional)
- Large needle and strong thread
- Latex adhesive
- Dressmaker's pins

KEY
A = 46 in. (115 cm)
B = 30 in. (75 cm)
C = 2 in. (5 cm)

SPECIFICATIONS

Rug size: 46 x 30 in. (115 x 75 cm)
Technique: Prodding (see page 17)

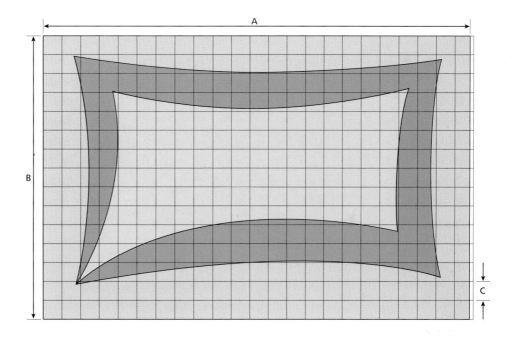

1 Prepare one blanket at a time. Cut the seams off the blanket, then cut it into 18-in. (45 cm) squares. Machine-wash to remove impurities. In a large pan, make up a solution of mauve dye according to the manufacturer's instructions, then dye two or three pieces of the blanket squares at a time. Each time a batch of dyeing is completed, color will be extracted from the solution. This will give a variety of shades. Use the dark green and pale green dye solutions in the same way on each of the other two blankets.

2 Using the sewing machine, overlock- or zigzag-stitch all around the raw edges of both pieces of the burlap to prevent it from fraying.

3 Using the marker pen, draw a 46 x 30 in. (115 x 75 cm) rectangle on one of the pieces of burlap, following the grainline and leaving a hem allowance of 3 in. (7.5 cm) on all sides.

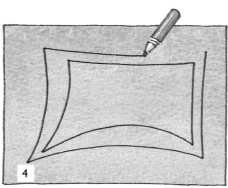

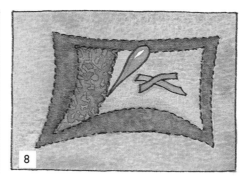

4 Referring to the diagram on page 27, use the tape measure and graph paper to draw the design onto the burlap. Attach the burlap to the frame, making sure that it is taut.

5 Using scissors or the rotary cutter and cutting mat, cut the dyed fabric into strips ½ in. (1.5 cm) wide, then cut the strips into 3½ in. (9 cm) clippings. Prepare a sizeable amount of fabric in each color before you begin prodding.

6 Begin working on the right side of the burlap, which will be the back of the rug. Working on the outlines, use the prodding tool to make a hole.

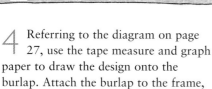

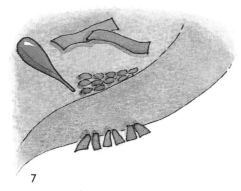

7

7 Push one of the strips of fabric halfway into the burlap with the prodder. Move along about three to four threads and make another hole. Push the other half of the fabric through with the prodder, using the fingers of one hand from behind the burlap to ensure that the ends are level. (The illustration shows what is happening on both the right side and the back of the rug.)

8 Make another hole three to four threads away and repeat the process. Continue working in this way, completing the outlines, then filling in the rest of the burlap with blocks of color, until all the prodding has been completed. Remove the rug from the frame.

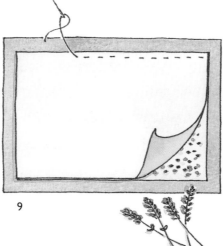

9

9 This step is optional. Lay a piece of interfacing on the back of the rug with the adhesive side facing upwards. Sprinkle the dried lavender flower heads evenly over the interfacing, then lay the second piece of interfacing on top of the seeds with the adhesive side facing down. Press according to the manufacturer's instructions. Secure the interfacing to the rug with running stitches.

10 Apply latex adhesive along a 3-in. (7.5 cm) border on the underside of the rug. Let it dry for a few minutes, then fold over the border to the underside of the rug, pressing the burlap down firmly and cutting off triangles at a 45-degree angle at the corners to achieve a neat, flat finish.

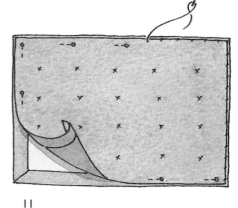

11

11 Lay the second piece of burlap over the back of the rug. Turning under a 3-in. (7.5 cm) hem all the way around, pin the burlap to the rug. Handsew the hem of the rug and the lining together with a strong thread in a matching color. Make small cross-shaped stitches at intervals over the back of the rug, sewing through the layers to hold them in place.

12 On the right side of the rug, trim the pile to an even height with a pair of sharp scissors.

Amish No. 4
Nicky Hessenberg

I have admired Amish designs and handicrafts for some years. The simplicity of the clear, uncluttered lines, the geometric shapes, and the color schemes convey the impression of a serene and orderly way of life. When looking through a book about Amish quilts, it occurred to me that many of the designs would transfer very successfully to hooked rag rugs. This is one of the designs I chose to adapt. I used two or three shades for each block of color. This was purely a personal decision and not a design necessity for making the rug.

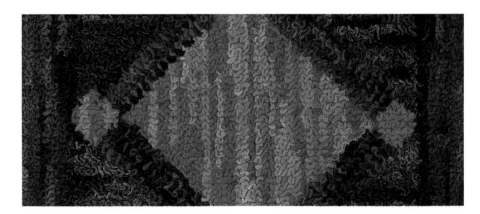

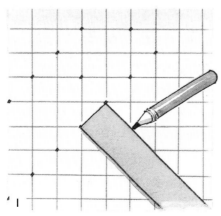

To neaten the rough edges at the top and bottom of the rug canvas, turn under a strip of three holes, making sure that the holes are in exactly the same place on both layers. Transfer the design onto the rug canvas freehand, using a steel ruler and a marker pen.

2 Cut the blanket fabric into strips about ¾ in. (1.5 cm) wide, using the rotary cutter and a cutting mat. Using the rug hook, pull a short strip of fabric through the canvas first to ensure that it is of the correct width to fill each hole in the weave. If it is not wide enough, it will slip out of the holes; if it is too wide, the canvas will become distorted.

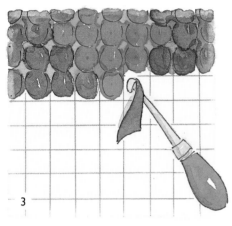

3 Using the rug hook, work the border first, starting in the middle of one side and working all the way around. Work along the rows, changing color wherever it is indicated on the pattern. When a strip is finished, pull the end to the front of the rug and start working with a new strip. Insert the new strip through the same hole as the end of the previous strip to ensure a firm fit.

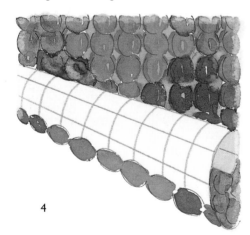

4 Check the underside of the canvas periodically to make sure that the loops are lying flat.

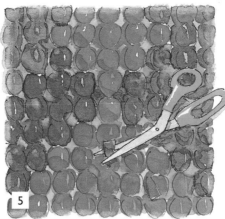

5 Once the pattern has been completed, trim the raw ends of the strips to the same height as the loops.

6 Place the rug on a blanket or some newspaper and spray it with water to 'set' the loops. Let it dry. If you want to give the rug an extra-firm backing, apply a weak solution of latex adhesive to the underside.

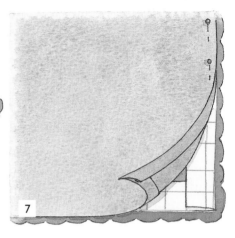

7 Turn under the two selvages on the edges of the canvas. Lay the rug face down on a flat surface and place the lining material on top of it. Turn the border under and pin the lining to the rug. Sew the backing to the rug with strong thread.

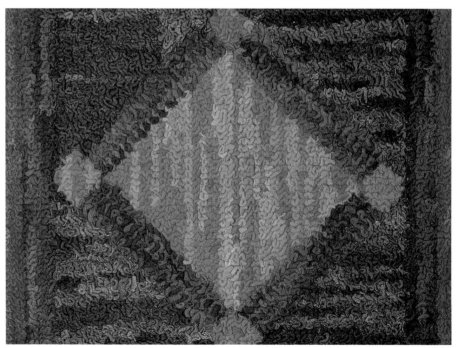

MAKER'S TIP

This rug is hooked with heavy wool blanket material that has been dyed and felted. Since the rag strips are so heavy, rug canvas has been used instead of burlap. The loft of the blanket wool holds the rags in place.

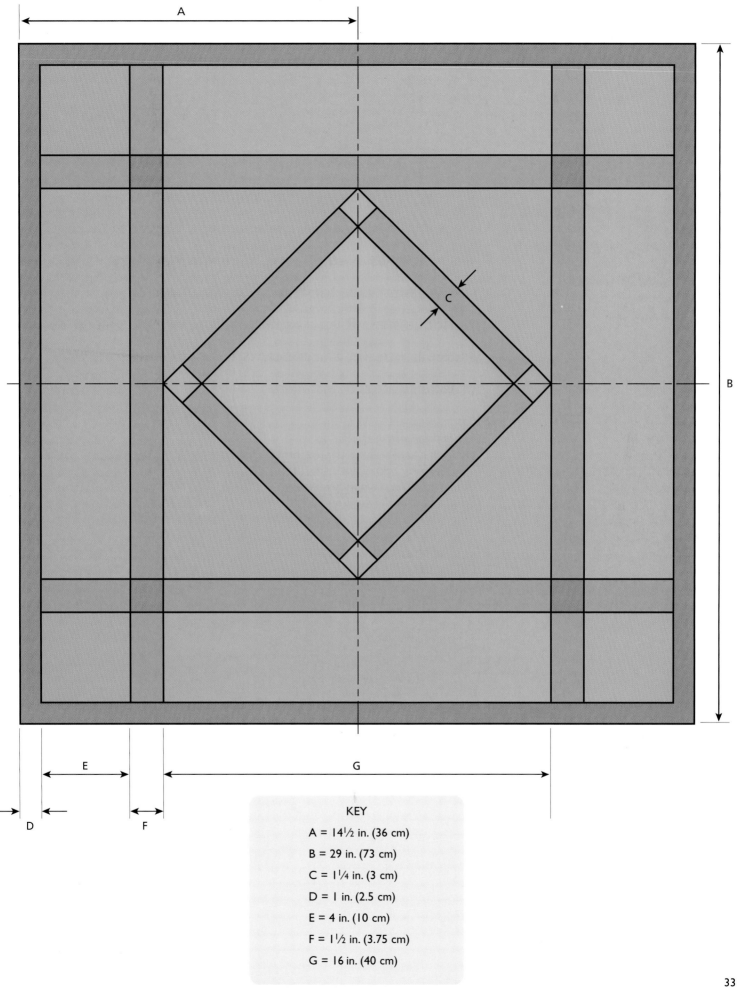

KEY

A = 14½ in. (36 cm)

B = 29 in. (73 cm)

C = 1¼ in. (3 cm)

D = 1 in. (2.5 cm)

E = 4 in. (10 cm)

F = 1½ in. (3.75 cm)

G = 16 in. (40 cm)

Cream Circle

Ann Davies
(Design by Piers Northam Interiors)

This rug, which is actually a sampler piece for a much larger rug, is so effective because of its elegant simplicity. I was commissioned to make it for a private customer. The rug was made for a bedroom in an apartment overlooking the River Thames, and the designer, Piers, wanted subtle yet warm shades to complement the furnishings already installed.

1 Find the center of the burlap by folding it into four equal parts, then mark the center with a dot, using the felt-tip pen. Place the burlap on a firm surface that will allow a pin to be pushed into it.

2 Measure and cut a piece of string 18 in. (45 cm) long.

3 Make a small knot at one end of the string and a loop at the other, making sure the string measures 16 in. (40 cm) in between. Push the felt-tip pen into the loop. Ensure that the pen is tightly held by the loop. Push the pin through the knot and pin it down into the burlap on the marked central point.

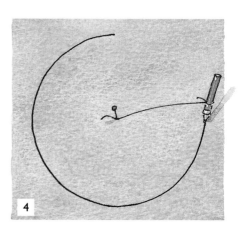

4

4 Use the string as a compass. Keep it taut and move the pen around the burlap, marking out a 32-in. (80 cm) circle; remove the pin and string.

5 Refer to the diagram on page 37. Measuring from the center, use a pencil to mark out a grid of 6-in. (15 cm) squares and 2-in.-wide (5 cm) bands on the burlap. Start by measuring 3 in. (7.5 cm) from the center mark in each direction and marking out that square first. To draw lines on the burlap, drag the pencil down toward you through two threads of the burlap, exerting slight pressure on the pencil tip to ensure that it drags down through the burlap in a straight line.

SPECIFICATIONS

Rug size: 32 in. (80 cm) in diameter
Techniques: Hooking (see pages 15–16), prodding (see page 17)

6 Attach the burlap to the frame, making sure that it is taut.

7 Using the rotary cutter and a cutting mat, cut the silk noil into ½-in.-wide (1 cm) strips, always cutting on the straight grain of the fabric, never on the bias.

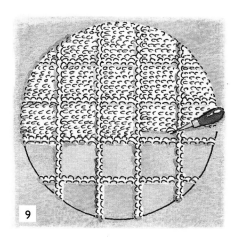

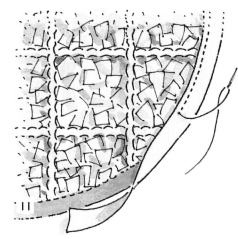

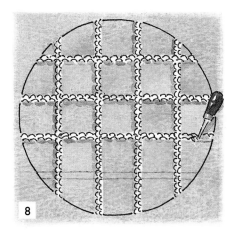

8 Work the hooked areas with the silk noil and a rug hook. These areas form a grid around the prodded squares.

9 Cut the cream wool flannel into ½ x 2¼ in. (1.5 x 6 cm) strips. Cut the pieces at an angle to the grain to create a varied look. Working on the reverse side, work the flannel into prodded areas in the grid formed by the hooking.

10 Take the piece from the frame and cut out the circle, leaving a border of about 1½ in. (4 cm) of burlap all around.

11 Simmer the carpet braid in a pan of hot water to allow for shrinkage, then dry and iron it. Using the strong cream thread, sew the braid firmly all around the front of the rug as close to the last row of work as possible. Use small, firm stitches, easing the braid slightly as you work. Leave a small piece of braid loose where you begin and end the stitching. When you have finished, turn under the ends of the braid and join them by butting them together with a stab stitch.

12 Before turning the braid down to stitch it to the burlap on the reverse side, snip the burlap at angles just short of where the braid is sewn on. This will enable the burlap to lie flat and the braid to be stitched down without distorting the circle.

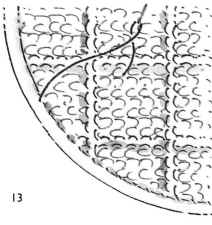

13

13 Stitch the braid to the reverse side, ensuring that it covers the snipped burlap completely.

14 Lay a towel on a flat surface. Place the rug on top with the reverse side facing up, then place a damp cloth on the hemmed-down braid and hold a hot iron to it. Use a pressing movement, not an ironing motion. Leave the rug to dry on the towel on a flat surface.

KEY
A = 3 in. (7.5 cm)
B = 2 in. (5 cm)
C = 16 in. (40 cm)

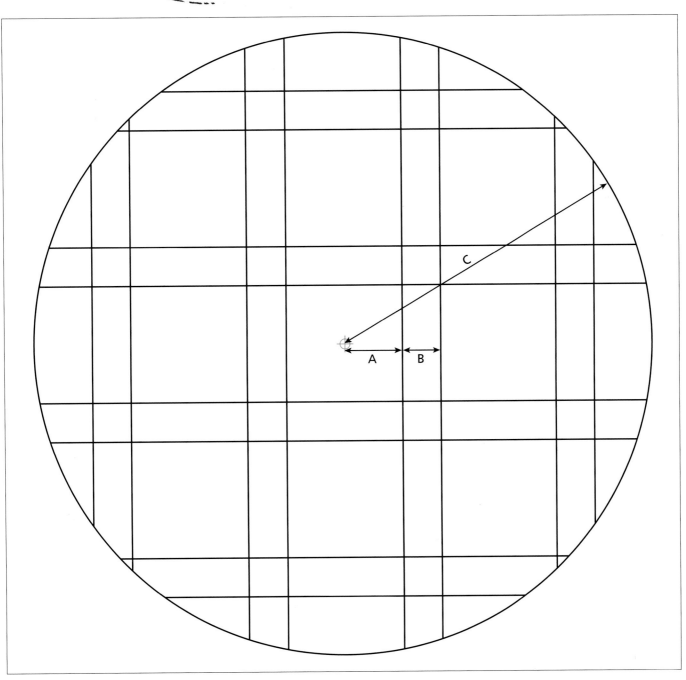

Color Stripes
Julia Burrowes

This clipped rug is very simple to make. It was inspired by the actual lattice marked out on the canvas.

I was interested in the secondary patterns that emerge whenever a set of rules are applied to a grid system.

I used a pale cream color for the background. For the dashes, you can use a random mix of colors or alternating colors, instead of sweeping bands of color as I have done.

I used canvas to make this rug because I feel that it is much stronger and easier to work with than burlap is.

It enables you to work from the front of the rug, allowing you to assess the piece as you progress. You can also take out and replace fabric strips in a canvas base as many times as you wish without causing any damage to the canvas. This encourages you to be much more adventurous in your work, as you can make adjustments, if required.

1 Referring to the diagram on page 40, measure out squares on the canvas, counting 10 vertical and 10 horizontal holes to each square. Outline the squares with a marker pen. (Some canvases have a grid of 3-in. (7.5 cm) squares already marked on them; if you have bought such a canvas, omit this step and use the existing squares as a guide.)

2 Draw alternating vertical and horizontal dashes in the center of each square as shown on the diagram.

A

B

C

3 Cut strips of fabric into short strips about 2½ in. (6 cm) long, using the rotary cutter and a cutting mat. The width of the strips will depend on the thickness of the fabrics you have chosen to use. Keep the different colored strips in separate piles.

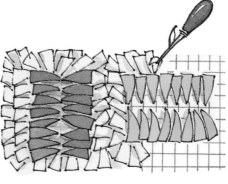

5

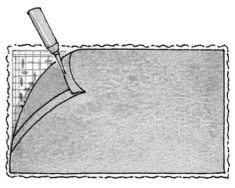

7

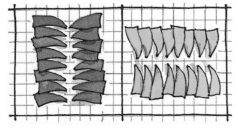

4

4 Using the spring clip tool, work the dashes first in the brightly colored fabric. Leave a row of holes at the top and bottom of each square, so that you clip eight strips of fabric for each stripe.

5 Fill in the remaining canvas, using pale cream or white strips of blanket fabric. Work in any direction that suits you, but make sure that no holes are left empty in the canvas.

6 When you have completed the rug design, turn it upside down and apply a coating of latex adhesive. Fold in the selvage edges and the top and bottom edges and glue them to the underside of the rug. Leave the rug to dry, preferably overnight.

7 Make the burlap backing. Turn a 2-in (5cm) hem of burlap to the inside and press it with an iron. Glue around the edges with the adhesive. Glue or stitch the burlap in place on the back of the rug.

8 Shake out the rug and trim the pile at the front. The more trimming you do, the clearer the design will appear, but you may prefer the shaggy effect of a longer pile.

> **MAKER'S TIP**
>
> *For a nonslip rug that can be placed on a polished floor, omit step 7 (attaching the burlap backing).*

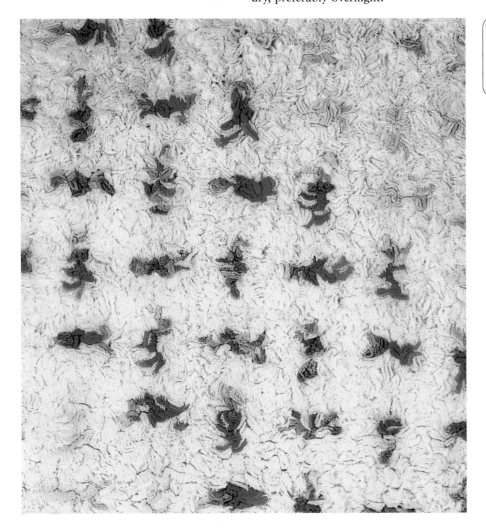

Braided Wool
Jenni Stuart-Anderson

- Scissors
- Selection of wool fabrics in gray, white, cream and black
- Long needle and gray thread
- Large safety pin
- Cup hook
- Dressmaker's pins
- Red fabric about 20 in. (50 cm) long (for binding)
- Red thread
- Backing fabric 32 x 20 in. (80 x 50 cm)

This simple, rustic rug is composed of chunky wool braids that have been left unplaited at the ends. I had originally planned for the rug to be monochromatic, but I decided to add a bright splash of red to enliven it. The materials used were cream and white blankets and black and gray coat and skirt fabrics. Because of the variations in the thicknesses of the fabric, I cut the thickest fabrics into strips roughly 2¼ in. (6 cm) wide, the medium ones into strips 2¾ in. (7 cm) wide and the thinnest ones into strips 4 in. (10 cm) wide. The plaits are sewn together to ensure that their weight does not pull them apart.

1 Using scissors, cut the fabrics into strips. If the fabrics are roughly the same weight and thickness, cut them into strips 2¼ in. (6 cm) wide. If they are different thicknesses, make a test braid to work out the thickness of the strips needed to make an even plait.

2 To make strips of fabric about 48 in. (120 cm) long, place two strips of the same fabric at right angles to each other. Stitch across the ends (by hand or by machine) at a 45-degree angle using the gray thread. Trim the seam to ¼ in. (5 mm) to make a smooth join.

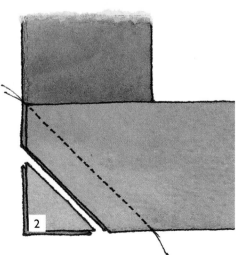

SPECIFICATIONS

Rug size: 30 x 18 in.
(75 x 45 cm)
Technique: Braiding
(see page 19)

3

3 Pin the ends of three 48-in. strips together with the safety pin, then hook the pin over a cup hook (or similar), attached to a firm surface that is roughly at eye level. Braid the strips, then secure both ends of the plait with a pin or a stitch. Make 10 more braids, using different combinations of fabrics.

4 Lay the plaits side by side and move them around until you like how they look. Try putting contrasting shades next to each other.

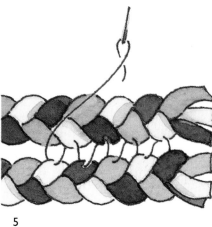

5

5 Place the first two plaits side by side with the ends level. With the needle and doubled gray thread, take a stitch from one plait, then make a stitch in the adjacent plait to join the two braids together. Continue stitching the plaits together, making sure that the thread will not be visible from the top of the rug. Work on a flat surface and do not pull the thread too tightly. Stop stitching 3½ in. (9 cm) from the ends and secure the braids firmly with a few extra stitches.

6 To strengthen the rug, turn to the back and oversew the join between the plaits with bigger stitches, which will be hidden by the backing and should not go through to the front. Sew the other plaits in the same manner, repeating steps 5 and 6.

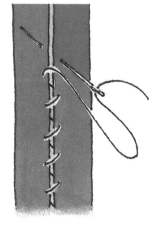

7

7 Cut strips of red fabric and join them into a strip three times the width of your rug. The width of this strip will depend on the weight of your chosen fabric. Use red thread to sew the long edges together to form a tube.

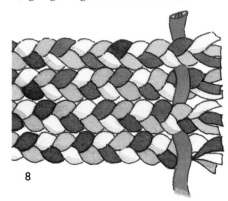

8

8 Weave the red fabric tube over and under the plaits at one end of the rug. When you get to the other side, secure the tube to the rug by stitching it, but do not pull the thread too tightly. Weave the tube back under and over the plaits until you reach the other side.

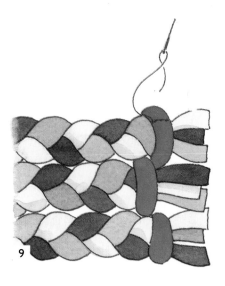

9

9 Before stitching the tube to the rug for the second time, loosen the ends of the braids so that they lie flat. Stitch the tube, trim off the excess, and conceal the end on the underside of the rug. Repeat these steps on the other end of the rug. Trim the unplaited 'fringe' at both ends of the rug so that it is even.

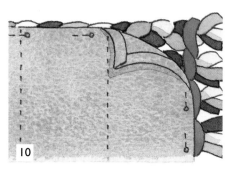

10

10 Place the backing fabric on the underside of the rug and turn under the edges by about 1 in. (2.5 cm). Pin the backing all the way around. Make sure that the backing is not visible from the front. Stitch the backing across the underside of the rug at right angles to the plaits in five evenly spaced, parallel lines. Use long, concealed stitches and small, visible ones. Then sew the backing to the rug around all the edges.

Sardines
Sara Worley

Childhood memories of exploring iridescent rock pools on Herne Bay beach in Kent, England, and having sardines on toast for afternoon tea inspired the design for this hooked rug. Make the design your own by drawing freehand the simple shapes, such as the spirals and stars. |If you want to make the rug even more original, make the outlines of the grid slightly irregular, as I have done here.

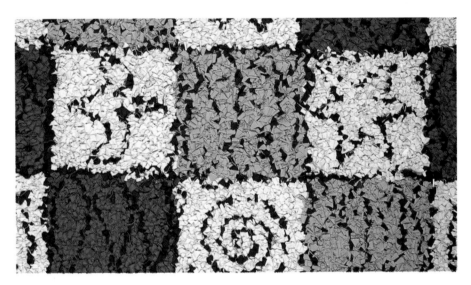

1 Enlarge the template on page 47 by 200%. Trace it onto tracing paper and transfer it onto the cardboard. Cut it out using a mat and a craft knife.

2 Using a tape measure and a steel ruler, measure and draw the grid of squares onto the burlap with a marker pen. Each square is 8 x 8 in. (20 x 20 cm). Measure out the border, which is 3 in. (7.5 cm) wide and draw it onto the burlap. Using the template, draw the fish in the squares, paying attention to how they overlap. Then draw the stars, spirals, and other designs freehand.

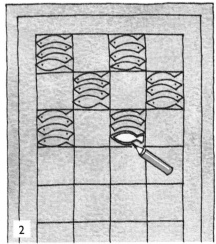

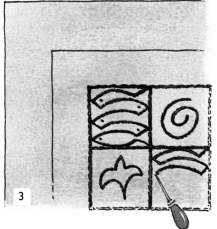

3

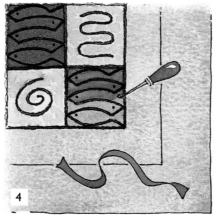

4

3 Attach the burlap to the frame, making sure that it is taut. Use a rug hook to hook in the strips of fabric, working all the black outlines first. If you would like to give the rug a handmade feel, make the outlines of the grid wavy.

4 Fill in the rest of the rug, hooking in the appropriate colors. When complete, remove it from the frame and place it face down on the floor. Turn in a double hem of about 2 in. (5 cm) and pin it all the way around. Sew the hem with wool thread, using a running stitch. Trim the pile with scissors.

KEY	
A = 38 in. (95 cm)	C = 8 in. (20 cm)
B = 54 in. (135 cm)	D = 3 in. (7.5 cm)

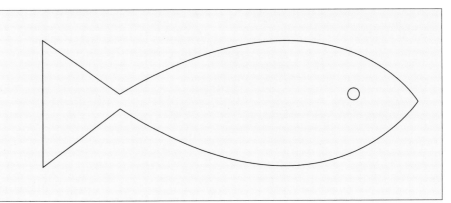

Shag Rag

Lizzie Reakes

Lizzie Reakes

You will need

- Steel ruler
- 10-oz. burlap 38 x 44 in. (95 x 110 cm)
- Permanent marker pen
- Scissors
- Selection of fabrics—velvet, printed cotton, knitted jersey, and wool
- 3 x 8 in. (7.5 x 20 cm) piece of thick cardboard
- Spring clip tool
- Dressmaker's pins
- Needle and strong linen thread

Although this clipped rug was made according to a traditional rag-rug technique, the bright, fresh colors give it a contemporary feel. Before starting to work the rug, I collected a variety of fabrics in different shades of red and green, including old printed cottons, chunky wools, lush velvets, knitted jerseys, and worn tartans, and cut them into strips.

1 Using a steel ruler, measure a border area of 4 in. (10 cm) inside the burlap. Outline it with a marker pen. You should now have a rectangle measuring 30 x 36 in. (75 x 90 cm) marked on the burlap. Unlike the other projects in this book where burlap is used as the base fabric, I did not use a frame. However, there is no reason why you cannot work the rug on a frame if your prefer.

2 With scissors, cut the fabrics into rectangles measuring about 1½ x 6 in. (4 x 15 cm). To do this, I find it best to cut a length of fabric 1½ in. (4 cm) wide (the strip should be as long as possible). Wind the fabric around a thick piece of cardboard (using the shortest side of the cardboard as your measurer). Cut along the top of the cardboard to make several rectangular clippings at once.

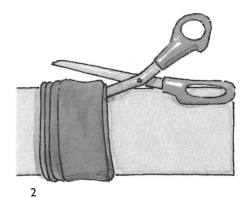

2

3 Repeat this process with all of the fabrics until you have enough to fill in the burlap. You will need approximately 1,720 clippings (860 in each shade, using a selection of fabric textures for both colors).

SPECIFICATIONS

Rug size: 30 x 36 in. (75 x 90 cm)
Technique: Clipping (see page 18)

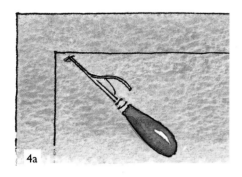

4a

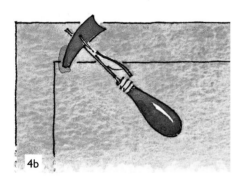

4b

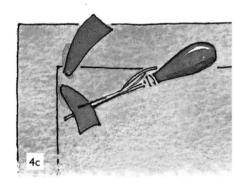

4c

4 Using the spring clip tool, begin clipping inside the top left-hand corner of the rectangle, working down the shorter side. Push the spring clip tool through the burlap, open the hinge, and attach the short end of the clipping into the tool. Release the lever handle to close the tool (4a). Pull the clipping halfway through the burlap (4b). Measuring down approximately ¾ in. (2 cm), push the spring clip tool through the burlap and pull through the other end of the clipping (4c).

5 Continue working down the row until it is filled. For the next row select a different color in a variety of shades and textures. Continue until the rectangular area is filled, varying the shades and textures as you go.

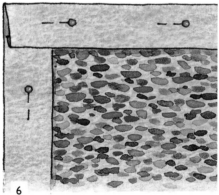

6

6 Once the clipping is complete, turn the rug face down on a flat surface and trim the frayed edges of the burlap. Pin back a hem of 4 in. (10 cm) around the rug. Using a needle and strong linen thread, stitch the hem onto the back of the rug.

MAKER'S TIP

This method of clipping is slightly different from that shown on page 18. The result is exactly the same, so just work in the way that is most comfortable and quickest for you.

Canyon
Sara Worley

You will need

- Dressmaker's pins
- 10-oz. burlap 40 x 58 in. (100 x 145 cm)
- Needle and strong thread
- Tape measure
- Steel ruler
- Marker pen
- Frame
- Rug hook
- Selection of cotton and cotton/polyester fabrics cut into strips
- Large-eyed needle and wool thread
- Scissors

The design for this simple, geometric hooked rug was influenced by the adobe buildings and monumental canyons of the southwestern United States. Only four colors of fabrics were used to make the rug — red, brown, cream and black — although the shades within those colors vary slightly in order to create a vibrant feel.

1 Pin a 2-in. (5 cm) hem around all the sides of the burlap, then sew it in place with strong thread.

2 Referring to the diagram on page 53, use a tape measure, steel ruler, and marker pen to measure and draw out the grid of squares (each square is 9 x 9 in./23 x 23 cm).

> ### SPECIFICATIONS
> *Rug size:* 27 x 45 in.
> (68 x 113 cm)
> *Technique:* Hooking
> (see pages 15–16)

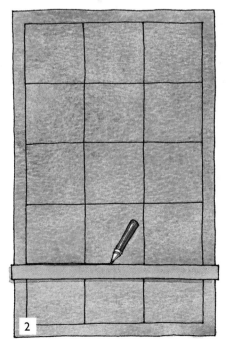

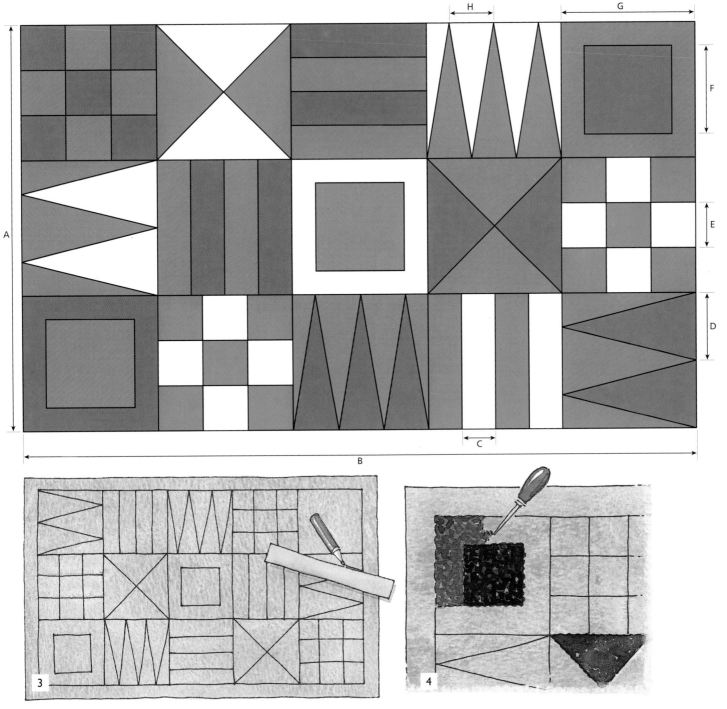

3 Draw the patterns on each square, either freehand or using a ruler.

KEY

A = 27 in. (68 cm)	E = 3 in. (7.5 cm)
B = 45 in. (113 cm)	F = 6 in. (15 cm)
C = 2¼ in. (5.75 cm)	G = 9 in. (23 cm)
D = 4½ in. (11.5 cm)	H = 3 in. (7.5 cm)

4 Attach the burlap to the frame, making sure that it is taut. Use a rug hook to hook the strips of appropriately colored fabrics into each square, building up the design. This is best done color by color. Continue doing this until the rug is complete.

5 Remove the rug from the frame and place it face down on the floor. Fold the unworked burlap to the underside of the rug and pin it all the way around. Fold and pin the corners neatly. Sew the hem to the back of the rug with wool thread, using a running stitch. Trim the pile with scissors.

Chevrons
Julia Burrowes

Using a very simple design like this one allows me to incorporate certain aspects of the interior decor into the rug. I have made many variations of this design and they all look completely different. The background for this geometric clipped rug was made from a variety of pastel-colored wool fabrics, which I obtained from an assortment of old felted sweaters. I also used dyed blanket fabric to extend the color range. Plain cream blanket fabric was used for the chevrons. You can use any color scheme of your choice.

1 Referring to the diagram on page 57, use a ruler to measure squares on the canvas, counting 10 vertical and 10 horizontal holes to each square. Outline the squares with a marker pen. (If you are using a canvas with a grid of 3-in./7.5 cm squares marked on it, omit this step and use the existing grid.

2 Enlarge the template on page 56 by 200%, then enlarge this copy by 180%. Place the template on a piece of cardboard. Using a craft knife, a metal ruler, and a cutting mat, cut around the rectangular shape and cut out the four 'windows' forming the shape of two chevrons.

3 To begin marking out the chevrons, position the bottom left-hand corner of the template at the bottom left-hand corner of the canvas and trace around the four shapes with the marker pen. Slide the template upward until the bottom two windows are aligned with the top two chevrons you have just

drawn. Make sure you keep the left-hand side of the template aligned with the edge of the canvas. Trace around only the top two windows this time.

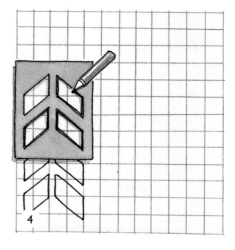

4 Slide the template upward again until the chevrons that you have just drawn appear in the bottom two windows. Trace around the top two windows again and repeat this process until you reach the top of the canvas.

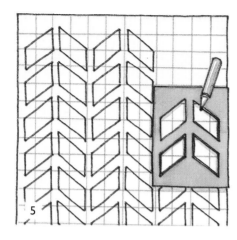

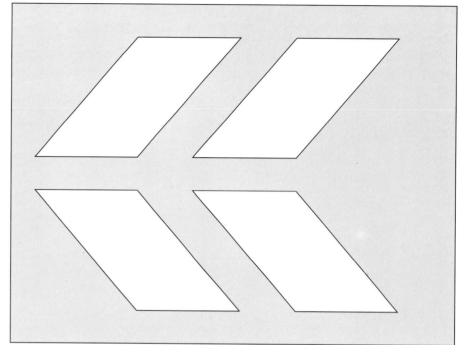

5 To draw the second and third rows of chevrons, start with the bottom edge of the template aligned with the bottom of the canvas and the left-hand edge of the template aligned with the right-hand side of the chevrons of the previous row. Repeat the process as described in steps 3 and 4 until there are three rows of chevrons covering the canvas. The partial chevron shapes at the bottom of the canvas can be constructed using the template and working downward from the first shapes drawn.

6 Using a rotary cutter and a cutting mat, cut the fabric into short strips about 2½ in. (6.5 cm) long. The width of the strips will depend on the thickness of the fabrics you use. Mix the colored strips together in a large pile in order to achieve a random color effect in the mat. Keep the cream blanket fabric strips separate from the colored strips.

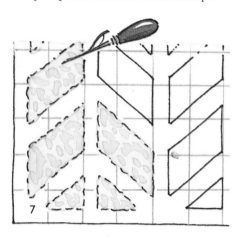

7 Using the spring clip tool, work the chevron shapes first in the cream blanket fabric.

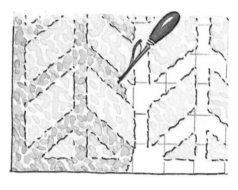

8

8 Fill in the vertical and diagonal lines between the chevrons with the colored strips. Work in any direction that suits you, but make sure that no holes are left unfilled in the canvas.

9 When complete, turn the rug upside down and apply a coating of latex adhesive. Fold in the selvages and the top and bottom edges of unworked canvas, and glue them to the back. Leave the rug to dry overnight.

10 Make the burlap backing. Turn the excess burlap to the inside and press it with an iron. Glue around the edges with the adhesive. Glue or stitch the burlap in place on the back of the rug. Omit this step if you want a rug with a nonslip backing.

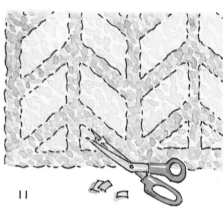

11

11 Shake out the rug and trim the pile at the front of the rug, using a pair of sharp scissors. Cut carefully until you achieve the effect you like—you may want to leave the pile quite long for a shaggy effect.

A

B

C

KEY
A = 36 in. (90 cm)
B = 60 in. (150 cm)
C = 3 in. (7.5 cm)

Tulips
Diana Woods-Humphery

Diana Woods-Humphery

You will need

- Large piece of paper 52 x 34 in. (130 x 85 cm)
- Masking tape
- Rug canvas 50 x 32 in. (125 x 80 cm)
- Marker pen
- Tracing paper
- Piece of lightweight cardboard 15 in. (38 cm) square
- Heavy-duty scissors
- Enough burlap to make three 15-in. (38 cm) square pieces
- Circular embroidery frame about 8 to 10 in. (20 to 25 cm) in diameter
- Rug hooks (1 small, 1 large)
- Red closely woven fabric (e.g. jacket material) cut into ½-in.-wide (1 cm) strips
- Latex adhesive
- Blue knitted fabric
- Large pins
- Needle and button thread
- Wool thread
- Cream blanket fabric cut into ¾-in.-wide (1.5 cm) strips
- Dark woven wool, such as skirts, trousers, or jackets, cut into ¾-in.-wide (1.5 cm) strips
- Spring clip tool
- Burlap for backing, 50 x 32 in. (125 x 80 cm)
- Iron

SPECIFICATIONS

Rug size: 48 x 30 in. (120 x 75 cm)
Techniques: Hooking (see pages 15–16), clipping (see page 18)

This rug was designed for a bedroom that has a Rennie Mackintosh (Scottish architect, designer, and artist, 1868-1928) theme. The rug incorporates the techniques of hooking, clipping, and wrapping. It is worked for the most part on rug canvas, which was chosen because it is taut and does not need a frame. The stems for the tulips are made from rolled pieces of fabric that are wrapped with wool thread to secure them. The tulip heads are worked separately with a small hook onto squares of burlap, which allows for fine hooking to provide more detail. The darker areas of the rug are worked predominantly in black, but they can be made more interesting by working in a variety of dark, woven wool fabrics, such as tweed.

1 Referring to the diagram on page 61, draw a full-size template of the design on a large piece of paper. Make sure that the pattern stands out well.

2 Apply a length of masking tape over the raw edges of the canvas to protect them. Place the canvas on the template and weigh it down so that it cannot move (any small, heavy household object will do; I use old, cast-iron weights from kitchen scales or old flat irons). Because the canvas has a very open weave, you can trace the design onto it directly from the template underneath, using the marker pen.

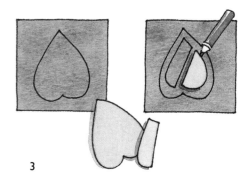

3 Make templates for the tulip heads. Trace a tulip head from the main design onto tracing paper, then transfer it to the cardboard. Cut out three pieces for the tulip head: one for the overall shape and two for the red areas. Outline the tulip heads on the three squares of burlap by drawing around the templates with the marker pen.

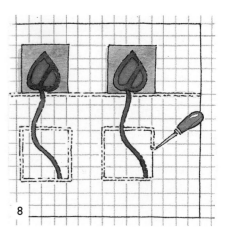

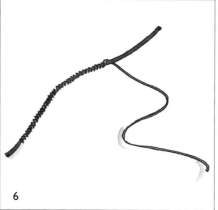

4 Work the three tulip heads first. Secure each piece of burlap in turn in the embroidery frame and, using the smaller hook, hook ½-in.-wide (1 cm) strips of red fabric.

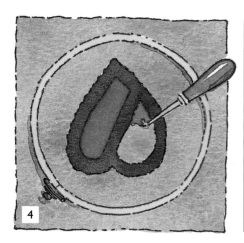

5 Cut out the tulip heads, leaving a margin of about 1½ in. (4 cm) of unworked burlap all the way around. Glue the motifs to the canvas, using the latex adhesive quite generously under the area you have worked. When you clip the background around the motifs, you will need to work into the burlap border as well as into the rug canvas. This may be hard work, but it will ensure that the motifs are anchored neatly and securely.

6 To make the stems for the tulips, roll a piece of blue knitted fabric about 20 x 7 in. (50 x 18 cm) long into a tight tube. Make sure that the tube is thin enough to make a convincing stem for the tulip, then pin and handsew it, using the button thread, down the long, rough edge. Wrap the stem with wool thread, leaving an unwrapped margin at the top and bottom. (In this case, I used matching wool, but you could experiment with contrasting colors.)

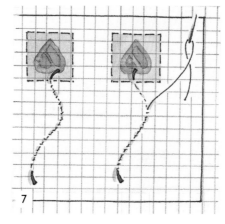

7 Push the unworked ends of the tube through to the back, where you will later sew them down neatly. Where the stem meets the tulip head, you will have to ease enough space in the burlap border to get the stem through to the back. Pin the stem into place, then turn the work over. Working down the back of the stem, sew it firmly into place with the button thread. Repeat these steps for the other two stems.

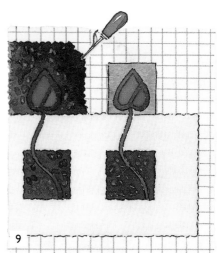

8 Most of the rug is worked with the spring clip tool, although certain lines are hooked to give definition. Using long strips of cream blanket material about ¾ in. (1.5 cm) wide, hook a row of strips at what will be the top of the main cream area and around the three rectangles. Then hook a row of dark fabric against the cream ones.

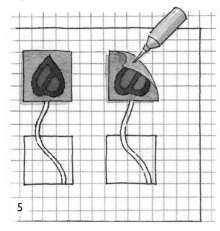

9 Fill in all of the remaining areas with the spring clip tool, using pieces measuring about 3¼ x 2¼ in. (1.5 x 6 cm). Work up to the selvages of the canvas on the long sides, using the spring clip tool. Where you have covered the ends of the canvas with masking tape (which should be removed at this stage), turn these under the width of three small squares and work through the double thickness of the canvas to neaten the edges.

10 Using the spring clip tool will give a shaggy effect to the rug. You may be pleased with this or you might prefer to shear and sculpt the pile for a more refined effect. Hold the rug over your knee and start to shear carefully with a pair of heavy-duty scissors. You will find that this produces further patterns and more texture. I sheared a little more around the edges and also where the color changes from dark to light in order to give the large areas a slightly cushioned effect. Avoid cutting too deeply into the clipping in any one place. Aim to cut the large areas of clipping to the same height, except at the edges.

11 Turn the rug face down and sew down the ends of the tulip stems. Apply latex adhesive to the back of the rug. Affix the selvages and secure the corners neatly. Leave the rug upside down until it is dry.

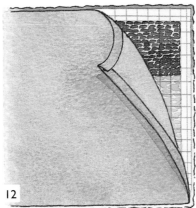

12 For the backing, cut the burlap about 2 in. (5 cm) larger than the rug overall, turn the excess to the inside, and press it with an iron. Glue around the edges with the adhesive. Place the wrong side down on the back of the rug, then iron the center with a moderately hot iron so that it starts to weld to the original latex adhesive finish.

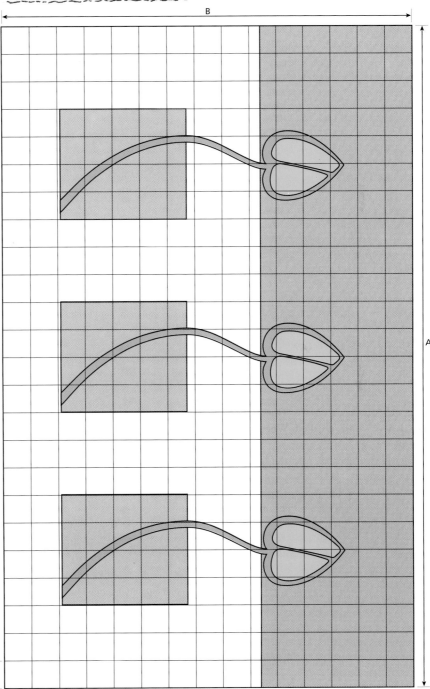

KEY

A = 48 in. (120 cm)

B = 30 in. (75 cm)

C = 2 in. (5 cm)

Little Rascals
Lizzie Reakes

Lizzie Reakes

The inspiration for this rug came from our much-loved family pet Jack Russells, Squirt and Joe. A palette of varying shades of primary colors, combined with complementary tones to highlight the pattern, was used for the design. I also used a wide selection of fabrics in a variety of textures. These included cotton, wool, knitted jersey, and crimplene. To depict the dogs' personalities, I introduced elements of appliqué within the hooked areas. Buttons were used to highlight the dogs' features, such as the eyes and noses, and also to decorate the collars.

1 Referring to the diagram on page 65, draw the design onto the burlap with a marker pen. You may want to draw a grid onto the burlap to help you. Allow for a border area of 4 in. (10 cm).

2 Select the fabrics and, using the rotary cutter and cutting mat, cut them into strips about ½ in. (1 cm) wide and as long as possible.

3 Using the staple gun, attach the burlap to the frame, making sure that it is taut.

> **SPECIFICATIONS**
>
> *Rug size:* 24 x 48 in. (60 x 120 cm)
> *Technique:* Hooking (see pages 15–16)

4 Work the appliquéd elements of the design first. To make the flower, sew the silk petals in a flower shape onto a circular piece of cotton material with a diameter of approximately 5½ in. (14 cm). To finish the flower, sew a button in the center. Sew this motif onto the burlap, leaving a gap of 1 in. (2.5 cm). Fill the space with the nylon stuffing and sew up the gap.

5 Using scissors, cut out the initials from old t-shirts, leaving a 1-in. (2.5 cm) border. To prevent fraying, turn under the border, then pin and sew it. Pin each rectangular initial into place on the burlap and stitch around each shape, leaving a 1-in. (2.5 cm) gap. Fill it with the nylon stuffing, then sew up the gap.

6 Using a rug hook, begin by hooking a dark color around the outside of the dog on the left-hand side. Then fill in the dog's body, using a selection of fabrics in different tones and textures to give the impression of fur.

7 For the eyes, select a large, pale-colored button and place a darker, contrasting-colored button on top, then sew them into position. By using mismatching buttons you can create more character around the eyes. You can also use buttons to highlight the nose areas and to emphasize the collars.

8 Continue working outward, hooking the background predominantly in red hues and

adding contrasting colors to achieve a painterly effect. For the border, use mainly blues and greens to make a surrounding frame of color.

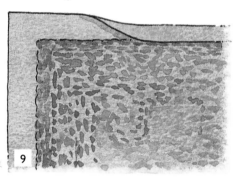

9 Once the hooking has been completed, remove the rug from the frame. Place the rug face down on a flat surface. Trim around the outer frayed edges with scissors. Apply a layer of latex adhesive around the burlap border. Wait 3 to 5 minutes, then turn in the edges and trim the excess fabric at the corners. Leave the rug to dry.

10 For the backing, pin the burlap to the back of the rug, then turn the excess backing fabric under all around and pin it. Stitch the backing into position using strong linen thread.

Sun Rays
Julia Burrowes

You will need

- Rug canvas 60 x 36 in. (150 x 90 cm)
- Steel ruler
- Marker pen
- Selection of fabric in shades of black and dark turquoise
- Selection of fabric in bright, vivid colors
- Rotary cutter
- Cutting mat
- Spring clip tool
- Latex adhesive
- Burlap 60 x 40 in. (150 x 100 cm) (optional)
- Iron
- Large needle and strong thread (optional)
- Scissors

This bright rug needs two base colors – I used shades of black and dark turquoise. It also requires a selection of bright, vivid colors. I obtained most of these from discarded wool dresses, but you could dye old wool blankets if you have them. I use Dylon dyes because they produce good results on a range of different fabrics. To obtain really vivid color, use natural fabrics, such as cotton and wool.

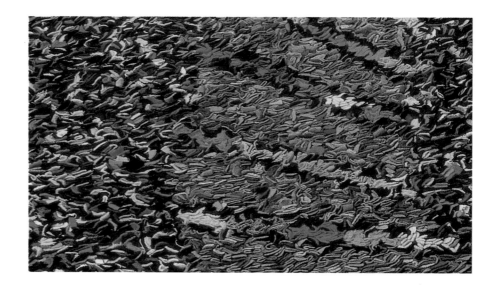

1 Referring to the diagram on page 68, measure squares on the canvas, counting 10 vertical and 10 horizontal holes for each square. Outline the squares with a ruler and a marker pen. (Omit this step if the canvas already has 3-in./7.5 cm squares marked on it and use them as a guide.)

2 Following the diagram, draw the design freehand, using the ruler and marker pen.

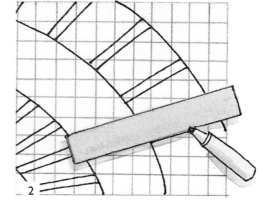

SPECIFICATIONS

Rug size: 56 x 36 in.
(140 x 90 cm)
Technique: Clipping
(see page 18)

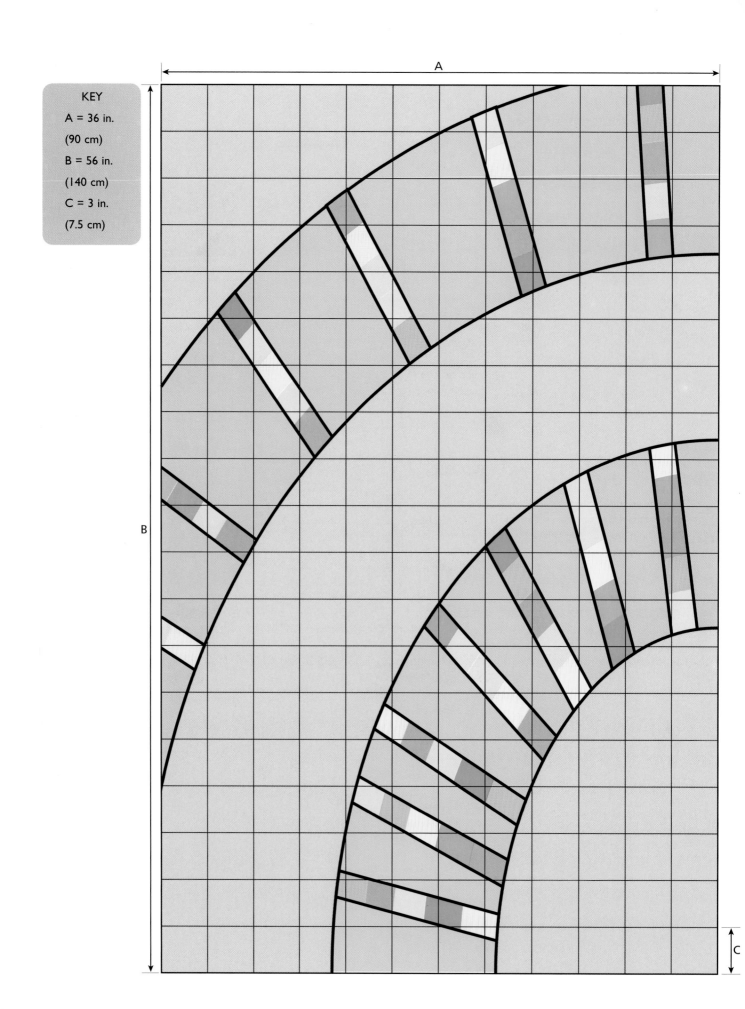

KEY

A = 36 in.
(90 cm)
B = 56 in.
(140 cm)
C = 3 in.
(7.5 cm)

A

B

C

3 Cut fabric into short strips about 2½ in. (6.5 cm) long, using the rotary cutter and cutting mat. The width of the strips will depend on the thickness of the fabrics you use (you need to keep the tension in the rug reasonably even). Prepare separate piles of strips in black and turquoise, then cut up the brightly colored fabrics and make a random mix of them. Add other colors until you achieve a mixture that you like.

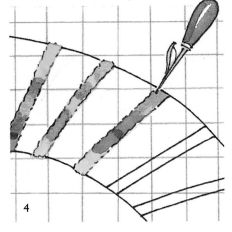

4 Using the spring clip tool, work the bands contained within the turquoise strips first. The bands need to be worked on the diagonal, which can be a little confusing. They may look slightly odd at this stage – if necessary, they can be adjusted as described in step 8 once the rest of the design has been filled in. Work as closely as possible to the drawn lines. Fill in the bands with narrow blocks of bright color. Work the blocks in varying lengths to achieve a random effect.

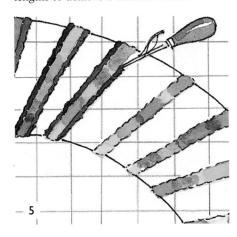

5 At the sides of each band, clip double-width rows of black fabric as outlines.

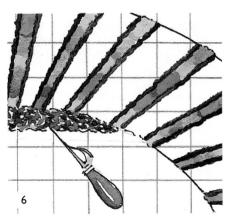

6 Fill in the three dark semicircular strips. Alternate the base color with a bright color until you have filled a line. Start the next line underneath, making sure that a bright color is placed under the base color. This will prevent stripes from forming.

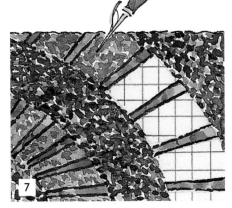

7 Fill in the segments between the bands with the turquoise fabric. If you are using a mixture of colors, avoid the colors that you have already used; this prevents the design from disappearing.

8 You may have to make a few small adjustments to the bands of bright color at this stage. If you have not kept the tension absolutely even, the bands may look a little wobbly. You can work fabric strips into thinner areas, and remove, reduce, and replace strips in areas that are too wide.

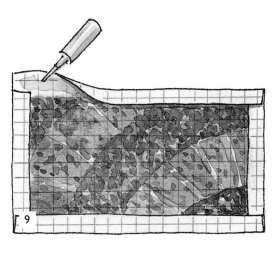

9 When finished, turn the rug upside down and apply a coating of latex adhesive. Fold in the selvage edges and the extra canvas at the top and bottom, and glue them to the back. Leave the rug to dry, preferably overnight.

10 Make the burlap backing. Turn the excess burlap to the inside and press it with an iron. Glue around the edges with the adhesive. Glue or stitch the burlap in place on the back of the rug. Omit this step if you want a rug with a nonslip backing.

11 Shake the rug to raise the pile and trim the rags using sharp scissors.

MAKER'S TIP

When trimming this rug, I suggest that you trim it quite closely, as the design will be much clearer if the rug has a short pile.

Hearts & Tulips

Amanda Townend

You will need

- Marker pen
- 10-oz. burlap 44 x 35 in. (110 x 88 cm)
- Steel ruler
- Frame
- A variety of fabrics, such as gold netting; iridescent gold silk; bright yellow-gold satin; black, purple, gray, and blue t-shirt material; and matted wool fabrics
- Rotary cutter
- Cutting mat
- Rug hook
- Scissors
- Iron
- Dressmaker's pins
- Needle and strong thread

SPECIFICATIONS

Rug size: 32 x 23 in.
(80 x 57 cm)
Technique: Hooking
(see pages 15–16)

I worked this brightly colored hooked rug in a variety of fabrics, including gold-sequinned netting from a 1950s ball gown, silvery gold silk from a favorite old skirt, and bright yellow-gold satin fabric that was used for curtains in the 1920s. The background to the design was worked predominantly in black, although many different shades of purple, gray, and blue fabrics were mixed into it.

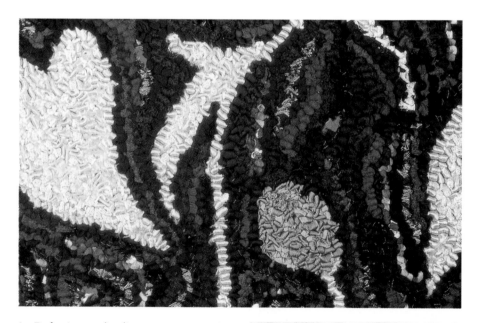

1 Referring to the diagram on page 72, use a marker pen to draw the design freehand onto the burlap or outline a grid with a ruler, if you prefer. Attach the burlap to the frame, making sure that it is taut.

2 Cut the fabric into strips, using the rotary cutter and cutting mat. Vary the width of the strips according to the fabric you are using.

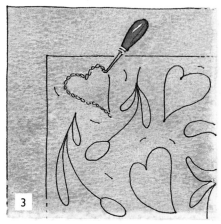

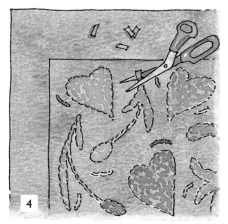

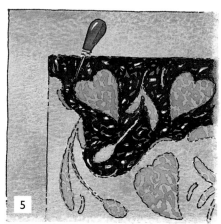

3 Using a rug hook, begin by hooking a motif on the left-hand side of the burlap. Fill in each shape before filling in the background.

4 Trim the end of each strip to the same level as the hooked loops.

5 Fill in the entire background. Once you have finished hooking, remove the rug from the frame, then, using an iron, press it gently with an iron on the wrong side. Turn the unworked burlap edges to the back of the rug, turn under the raw edges, pin them in place, and sew the hem with strong thread. Give the underside of the rug a final press.

KEY

A = 32 in. (80 cm)

B = 23 in. (57 cm)

C = 1½ in. (4 cm)

Sleight
Julia Burrowes

You will need

- Rug canvas 64 x 36 in. (160 x 90 cm)
- Steel ruler
- Marker pen
- Selection of fabrics in 5 different tones in a mix of colors
- Rotary cutter
- Cutting mat
- Acrylic paints in canary yellow, emerald green, crimson, ultramarine, and black
- Medium-size paintbrush
- Pencil
- Spring clip tool
- Scissors
- Latex adhesive
- Burlap 64 x 40 in. (160 x 100 cm) (optional)
- Iron
- Large needle and strong thread (optional)

SPECIFICATIONS

Rug size: 60 x 36 in.
(150 x 90 cm)
Technique: Clipping
(see page 18)

This clipped rug is so named because it is quite hard to follow the pattern exactly. Planes appear to shift backward and forward and above and behind each other, so that you cannot quite see what is going on at first glance. It is an ambitious piece and you will need to enjoy working with closely related colors and tones to achieve a convincing effect. The design is made from five batches of different colored strips that have been sorted into varying tones.

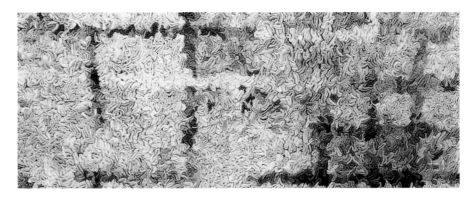

1 Referring to the diagram on page 76, measure squares on the canvas, counting 10 vertical and 10 horizontal holes to each square. Outline the squares with a ruler and a marker pen. (Omit this step if the canvas already has 3-in./7.5 cm squares marked on it and use these as a guide.)

2 Prepare a mixture of fabric strips in five different tones and a mix of colors. Using a rotary cutter and cutting mat, cut the strips into short clippings about 2½ in. (6.5 cm) long. The width of the strips will depend on the thickness of the fabrics you use.

Keep the strips in five separate piles of different tonal values, e.g. very pale, pale, medium, dark, and very dark.

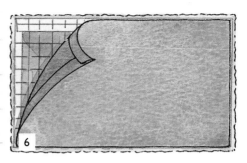

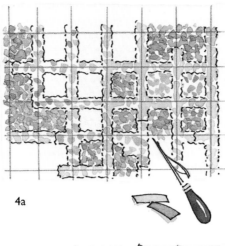

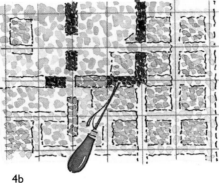

4a

4b

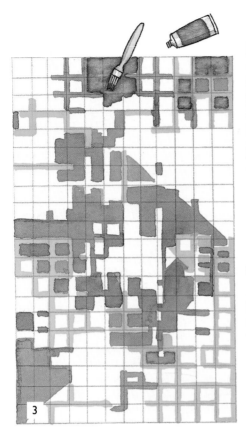

3

3 Following the diagram on page 76, use the acrylic paints and a brush to paint the design directly onto the canvas. Each color represents one of the five tones. If you lack confidence in painting the colors directly onto the canvas, first draw the outlines of the shapes with a pencil, then fill them in with paint. Wait until the paint is thoroughly dry before you start to work the canvas.

4 Using the spring clip tool, fill in the yellow areas with the selction of very pale colors, the green areas with the pale colors, the pink areas with the medium colors, the blue areas with the dark colors, and the black areas with very dark colors.

5 When you have finished, lightly trim the surface of the rug with scissors and check and adjust any irregular areas as necessary.

6 Turn the rug upside down and apply a coating of latex adhesive. Fold in the selvage edges and the extra canvas, top and bottom, and glue to the back. Leave the rug to dry overnight.

7 Make the burlap backing. Turn the excess burlap to the inside and press it with an iron. Glue around the edges with the adhesive. Glue or stitch the burlap in place on the back of the rug. Omit this step if you want a rug with a nonslip backing.

8 Shake out the rug and trim the pile at the front with a pair of sharp scissors. The more trimming you do, the clearer the design will appear, but you may prefer the shaggy effect of a longer pile.

MAKER'S TIP

This rug is made of rag strips in a mix of colors in five different tones. For the rug design to be effective, you need to identify these tones very carefully. One trick is to cut small strips of fabric, stick them onto a sheet of paper, and photocopy them. Discard any colors that appear to stand out too much. Another way is to look at a pile of fabric through half-closed eyes; any colors that do not mix in tone will stand out.

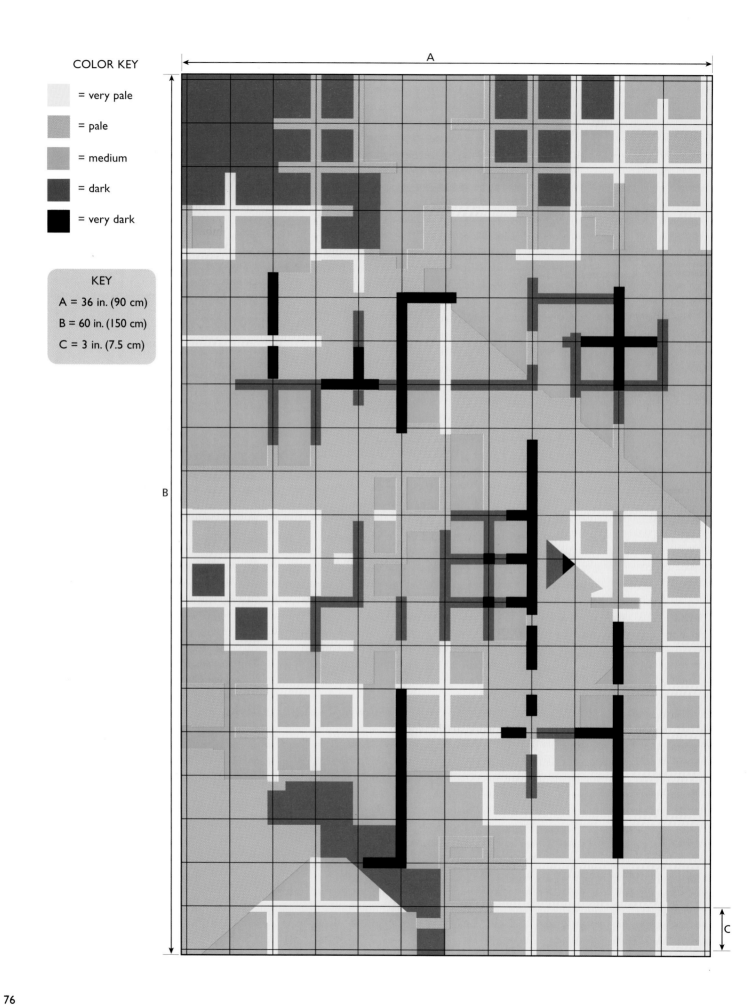

COLOR KEY

= very pale

= pale

= medium

= dark

= very dark

KEY
A = 36 in. (90 cm)
B = 60 in. (150 cm)
C = 3 in. (7.5 cm)

A

B

C

ABOUT THE CONTRIBUTORS

JULIA BURROWES has been teaching painting and the history of art at the same school for 23 years. When her children were young and she found that their demands, those of her job, and her other passion, horses, took up all of her time, she spent very little time doing her own work. It was always her intention to paint seriously again as soon as she had the time to concentrate properly. Then one day she decided to make a rag rug, like the ones she had seen in Yorkshire as a child, to replace one that had worn out. The rest is history. Julia feels that the beauty of rag-rug making is that it can be as simple or as complicated as you wish and still keep its integrity. You can virtually "paint with rags," as the effect is similar to pointillist painting.

Julia currently teaches rag-rug making at West Dean College, Chichester. She exhibits and has work in public and private collections in the UK and abroad. Julia accepts some commissions but there is a waiting list. She is a member of the 62 Group of Textile Artists.

ANN DAVIES' interest in the manipulation of fabrics stems from her training as an embroiderer. She has been involved in rag-rug making for nearly 40 years. During that time she has researched a variety of rug-making techniques, some well known, some not, which have formed the basis of the four books she has written on the subject.

During her association with this craft she has written and lectured in the UK and the USA. Her work is in various private collections in the UK, Italy, and the USA.

More than 40 years ago, MAUREEN GREEN watched her aunt make a prodded rug from old clothes and she remembers it as being dark and drab. Many years later she saw rug making demonstrated at a textile fair, where the crafter used beautiful materials in vibrant colors, and she was hooked! Maureen has been making rugs ever since.

She piloted a City and Guilds in rag-rug making at the Deighton Center, Huddersfield, and has recently completed an adult education teaching certificate. Her work at the Tolson Memorial Museum has given her the opportunity to promote her work through exhibitions and workshops. Maureen uses mainly recycled materials but does buy luxurious velvet remnants from her local mill; they are just too good to pass up.

NICKY HESSENBERG has been interested in working with textiles for many years. After taking a course in constructed textiles as an adult student, she developed an interest in the history and methods of making rag rugs. She learned the relatively simple techniques of prodding and hooking and started making her first rug using scraps of leftover fabric. Nicky likes the idea that rag-rug making does not have to be a solitary activity – the rug can be rolled up and taken anywhere; it then becomes a social activity as well as a creative one. She likes the idea of using recycled materials and very often uses fabrics that hold particular meaning. Nicky produces a wide variety of pieces, large and small. It is the creative freedom of rag-rug making that spurs her on to start the next project.

LIZZIE REAKES has been exhibiting her work both nationally and internationally since 1991. Her work is collected for private homes, museums, and galleries. Inspirational themes include football, family pets, and music. "There is a real challenge when using old and unwanted materials to transform and change their identity and character. I first explored rag-rug making as an art student and have continued ever since. I am inspired by traditional folk art images and commemorative text that appears on the surface pattern of historical rag rugs from Canada. I now combine appliqué with hooking to make logos, numbers, and symbols in my own work. I want my work to look drawn, painted, and handmade."

She lives with her husband and daughter in Hertfordshire and combines commissioned work with exhibitions, teaching, and lecturing throughout the UK.

JENNI STUART-ANDERSON worked as an architectural designer until the birth of her daughter in 1984. At home in rural isolation with her baby, she asked a friend, Mrs Tunley, who had made rag rugs for more than 50 years, to show her the traditional techniques. It was the ideal pursuit that could be picked up and put down at a moment's notice. Soon she was exhibiting rugs, and so many people asked her how to do it that she started holding workshops. She now teaches in schools and at day and weekend residential workshops in Herefordshire and beyond. She enjoys helping people explore their creativity.

Jenni makes commissioned rugs using hooking, prodding, and braiding techniques. She often includes stitching and found objects as well. She supplies handmade tools and kits, and she is experimenting with more three-dimensional work and garment making, all using recycled textiles.

AMANDA TOWNEND was a student in the Carpet and Textile Design course at Kidderminster and Wolverhampton Polytechnic and now runs a rug and carpet workshop in Manchester using recycled plastic and woven and knitted materials. Generations of her family in the northwest and northeast of England have always made rag rugs. She became involved in the 'Hooky Matters' and 'A Day in the Life' projects organized by Ali Rhind, which became a touring exhibition.

Amanda runs workshops for children; people with special needs; students; and community groups in schools, colleges, art galleries, and museums. She exhibits her work throughout England. With textile designer Ann Marie Cadman, she coordinates the 'Kaleidoscope' exhibition, a showcase for designer craftspeople in the northwest of England.

DIANA WOODS-HUMPHERY has always been interested in all forms of needlework, textile crafts, and the concept of recycling. The notion of transforming discarded clothing into something entirely new, beautiful, and useful seems to her truly irresistible. Diana cannot claim, in a romantic vein, to have learned the craft of rugging at her grandmother's knee. She had a chance to indulge her interest a few years ago when she went to a summer school at West Dean College and fell under the spell of the rag-rug artist Julia Burrowes. Subsequently, as a maker of soft furnishings, she has sometimes been called upon to create a rug for a client's interior design scheme.

SARA WORLEY drifted into making rugs after studying 3D Design at art school in Rochester, Kent. She loves their tactile quality, the endless design possibilities, and the ability to work within the confines of a very traditional structure.

Although Sara's work has been exhibited in galleries, she prefers to see her rugs in people's homes, as the notion of creating something that is unique, totally handcrafted, and useful is at the very center of her work.

Most of her rugs tend to be hand-hooked with a loop pile but, to Sara, technique is far less important than the designs themselves. She also feels that there is something undeniably quirky about spending weeks or months striving to create a work of art that is destined to be walked all over!

RESOURCES

SUPPLIERS

ALI STREBEL DESIGNS
Kindred Spirits
Dayton, Ohio
937-299-6388
www.kindredspiritsdesigns.com

ANDERSON HANDCRAFTED PRODUCTS
Leonardtown, Maryland
301-994-2262
www.andersonframe.com

THE CARON COLLECTION
Stratford, Connecticut
203-381-9999
www.caron-net.com

COLORS BY MARYANNE
Wrentham, Massachusetts
508-384-8188

CROSS STITCHERY AND MAIN STREET FRAMING
La Crosse, Wisconsin
888-907-7008
www.crossestitchery.com

DIFRANZA DESIGNS
North Reading, Massachusetts
978-664-2034
www.difranzadesigns.com

FORESTHEART STUDIO
Woodsboro, Maryland
301-845-4447
www.forestheart.com

FREDERICKSBURG RUGS
Hunt, Texas
866-934-6273
www.fredericksburgrugs.com

GOOD TIDINGS
Cranberry Township, Pennsylvania
724-776-5791
shirlet@zoominternet.net

HANDS ACROSS TIME RUG HOOKING STUDIO
Pugwash Junction, Nova Scotia
902-257-3435
handsacrosstime@yahoo.ca

HARRY M. FRASER CO.
Stoneville, North Carolina
336-573-9830
www.fraserrugs.com

HIGHLAND HEART HOOKERY
Halifax, Nova Scotia
902-445-4644
www.hookarug.com

HOOK-IT TALL TIMBERS
7733 Airy Hill Road
Chestertown, Maryland
410-778-4939
www.hookit-talltimbers.com

HOOKED TREASURES
Cherylyn Brubaker
Brunswick, Maine
207-729-1380
www.hookedtreasures.com

HURON SHORE WOOLENS
North Street, Michigan
810-985-6096

J. CONNOR HOOKED RUGS
Hiram, Maine
207-625-3325
www.jconnerhookedrugs.com

JANE OLSON RUG STUDIO
Hawthorne, California
310-643-5902
www.janelsonrugstudio.com

LITTLE QUILTS
Marietta, Georgia
770-578-6727
www.littlequilts.com

MILLER RUG HOOKING
Nancy Miller Quigley
Reno, Nevada
775-747-1234
millerrugs@aol.com

MOONDANCE COLOR COMPANY
Oakham, Massachusetts
508-847-7493
www.moondancecolor.com

NEW EARTH DESIGNS
Jeanne Benjamin
Brookfield, Massachusetts
508-867-8114
www.newearthdesignsonline.com

THE NICHE IN THE NOOK
Farmingdale, Maine
207-582-4990
www.thenicheinthenook.com

NORTH SHORE ISLAND TRADITIONS
Past & Present Rug Shop
902-963-2453
www.hookamat.com

NORTHWOODS WOOL
Cumberland, Wisconsin
715-822-3198
www.northwoodswool.com

OVER THE RAINBOW YARNS
http://stores.ebay.com/
Over-The-Rainbow-Yarns

RUG BRAIDING & HOOKING
WITH VERNA
Cox Enterprises
Verona Island, Maine
207-469-6402
www.vernarug.com

RUGMAKER'S HOMESTEAD
Rafter-four Designs
Cocolalla, Idaho
info@rugmakershomestead.com
www.rugmakershomestead.com

TOMORROW'S HEIRLOOMS
11310 Prairie Street
Allendale, Michigan
616-895-6378
thhkrugs@altelco.net

W. CUSHING & COMPANY
Kennebunkport, Maine
800-626-7847
www.wcushing.com

WHISPERING HILL FARM
Woodstock, Connecticut
860-928-0162
www.whispering-hill.com

WHITE CAT WOOL
Cotuit, Massachusetts
508-420-9888
www.whitecatwool.com

THE WOOL STUDIO
Sinking Spring, Pennsylvania
610-678-5448
www.thewoolstudio.com

YANKEE PEDDLER HOOKED
RUGS
Killingworth, Connecticut
860-663-0526
www.yankeepeddler.com

WEBSITES

THE RUG HOOKE'S NETWORK
www.rughookersnetwork.com

RUG HOOKING MAGAZINE
www.rughookingmagazine.com

GUILDS AND ORGANIZATIONS

ASSOCIATION OF TRADITIONAL
HOOKING ARTISTS (ATHA)
www.atharugs.com

INTERNATIONAL GUILD OF
HANDHOOKING RUGMAKERS
(TIGHR)
www.tighr.net

NATIONAL GUILD OF PEARL K.
MCGOWN HOOKCRAFTERS
www.mcgownguild.com

INDEX